# LAPSIT SERVICES FOR THE VERY YOUNG

## A How-To-Do-It Manual

## LINDA L. ERNST

*HOW-TO-DO-IT MANUALS
FOR LIBRARIANS*

*Number 48*

**NEAL-SCHUMAN PUBLISHERS, INC.**
New York, London

Published by Neal-Schuman Publishers, Inc.
100 Varick Street
New York, NY 10013

Printed and bound in the United States of America.

**Library of Congress Cataloging-in-Publication Data**

Ernst , Linda L .
   Lapsit services for the very young child : a how-to-do-it manual /
Linda L . Ernst .
      p.    cm. -- ( How-to-do-it manuals for librarians ; no . 48 )
   Includes bibliographical references and index.
   ISBN 1-55570 - 185 - X
   1.  Public libraries--Services to toddlers--United States .
  2 . Public Libraries--Services to infants--United States .
  3 . Children ' s libraries--Activity programs--United States .
  I . Title .  II . Series:
  Z718 . 1 . E75    1995
  027 . 62 ' 5 ' 0973-- dc20                      95 - 16177
                                                   CIP

For my daughter Jessica Lynn who really got me involved in this area of library service and my husband David.

# CONTENTS

Colophon

# ACKNOWLEDGMENTS

Thanks to the Children's Librarians of the King County Library System, Washington for their support, questions and willingness to develop this area of library service to children. The Parenting Pathfinder included in this text is provided by KCLS.

Thanks to my editor, Virginia H. Mathews, for her patience.

To Margaret Read MacDonald, Elizabeth Panni and Patty Drew. I give an extra measure of thanks for their willingness to share their knowledge, comments and needs. Also for believing not only a book like this is important in the field of children's library service but that I was the one who should do it.

Special thanks to my husband David and daughter Jessica for without them this book would never have become a reality.

# FOREWORD

Gradually we librarians are accepting our responsibilities to the youngest of our charges . . . infants and toddlers. Research has shown that early intervention is basic to the educational life of our nation's children and the public library too has a role to play in this very early childhood education. Throughout the country libraries are beginning to offer not only just pre-school storytimes, but toddler times, and even lapsit programs for the youngest of all. Of course an important element of these programs is the parent education which takes place. And so we see ourselves thrust into a new realm of services with new audiences which may leave us a bit uneasy.

For years I have been an advocate for the inclusion of parent education as a component of all pre-school storytimes. I insist that parents should be included in the storytime so that they may encounter fine materials and useful techniques and may share in the literary play which goes on with their children. In Linda Ernst's lapsit programs the parent becomes a prime receiver of the program's information. She repeats her fingerplays over and over until they can't forget them. She sends them off with packets of material to provide at-home reinforcement. She is in fact educating the parent to carry on the program's stimulating activities at home with their child. This parent education is important work and we all need to follow her lead.

To tell the truth, the thought of being faced with a dozen squiggling babies strikes a bit of terror into most of us. I resisted adding lapsits to my program schedule and was uneasy even with the under 2's. Over time Linda's constant encouragement and insistence has persuaded many of us at King County Library System to hesitantly begin adding programs for these younger audiences. She has put that sensible and insistent encouragement into print here. Perhaps many of you readers will find her as persuasive as we did and begin a program of Lapsits. The clear guidance she offers here should get you on your way. As Linda points out, you already are familiar with all of the materials you need to offer these new Lapsit programs. It is just a matter of applying your skills to a new audience . . . an audience which she insists will bring you no end of delight!

Margaret Read MacDonald,
Bothell Public Library
King County Library System

# INTRODUCTION

Like many other children's librarians, I ventured into my first toddler storytime for children ages 2 to 3 years old with great intrepidation. Preschool storytime with children ages three to five year olds had become routine and comfortable to handle. I had been doing this kind of programming for years, but the toddler age group? "They're so little!", I thought. "How can I share stories with the children if they won't even sit still!" Well, I survived the experience and now would not dream of excluding this age group from regularly scheduled library programing. Many libraries, if not most, offer toddler and preschool programs on a regular basis. The community at large has grown to expect programing for this preschool age group in American libraries today. In the past few years however, a new cry has been increasing in volume from the community. That is for the library to develop programs for an even younger library patron, the infant (newborn to 12 months) and the pre-toddler (ages 12 to 24 months). Imagine my anxiety when confronted with that proposal! To make it even more interesting, I was the one who proposed the initial program at my library. Yet here I am, stating that programs and services for the very young child, newborn to 24 months, deserve a place in the public library. How did I become a convert? I asked myself a few questions first, ones you might ask yourself.

How are children ages newborn to 24 months currently being served by the public library? What services/programs are offered by community agencies and what kind of response have they been getting? If there are programs offered outside the library and there are lengthy waiting lists for them, it can indicate that there is a demand for this service. What kinds of services should your library offer and how do you decide which ones to offer? What do you have to know about this age group so that you can interact with them? What kind of program can you create and how much time will it take to put it together? Why attempt another service? What do you do and how do you do it? How will you let people know what you are planning in this perhaps new area of service? Lots of questions. After a great deal of searching, gathering and interweaving of material, I developed a program that was flexible enough to meet the need as I saw it. By compiling this information I hope that you too will find this area of service less complicated than you first imagined. In fact, you probably know more than you realize and only need to adapt what you know to the age group you intend to serve. Best of all, the fun and rewards of working with this age group are amazing.

# PERSONAL BACKGROUND

It should be noted that I am not an early childhood educator. Children's literature classes emphasized materials, but not necessarily how to introduce these materials to children. In this instance, children who were so young they had no concept of what a book or story even was. Something happened in 1985 that compelled me to learn quickly. My daughter, Jessica, arrived two months early and her tiny body (2 pounds 13 ounces) was placed in an isolette to protect and sustain her. Separated by a wall of glass we touched the only way we could, verbally. I read stories to her, sang to her, and told her all the rhymes that I could remember. We brought her home four weeks later, four pounds. four ounces, and of course we kept on telling her stories. Now, in second grade Jessica is proudly mastering the skills of reading and writing herself, even conceding to read to me on occasion.

During the years between Jessica's birth and going to school I used books and looked for programs not as a children's librarian, but as a parent. It struck me how amazingly little was offered for the very young child and how long the waiting lists were for programs that were available. So Jessica and I played our own storytimes with fingergames, songs, and stories. For me, it was simple but then I discovered not everyone thought so. David, my engineer husband, was 40 when his daughter arrived and his background was in computers not storybooks. My going back to work added to the awareness of finding that "quality time" many parents seem determined to experience with their children. I began to search for materials that would help me as a parent understand my child's development, books she would enjoy, programs we could share together and ended up in the wonderful world of Lapsit where they all meet in exciting possibilities for library programing.

# 1 LIBRARIES AND LITTLE ONES TODAY

The family today seems to be placed under increasing stress from the world around it. The number of families where both parents work outside the home is increasing, the number of homeless families is on the rise, and the struggle to make ends meet seems to be getting harder everyday. Teenage parents are increasing in number with many singles deciding to raise their child on their own. It seems that parents are being bombarded with the message that their children need to begin their education as soon as possible. Fathers are taking a larger part in early childcare, yet are not quite certain what that role is supposed to be. Bookstores have shelves and shelves of parenting books, self help books, "how-to-do-it right" books, etc. All parents want the best for their child, yet are often overwhelmed by the materials and choices available to them or uncertain where to begin. The library can be the family's refuge and their resource.

By making a variety of materials available to the community, individuals are able to make choices as to what materials or programs meet their needs. Allowing outside agencies to display materials and conduct programs at the library enables the family to network with agencies that may be of service to them and perhaps be more accessible for the family to be involved in.

Families today often find it difficult if not impossible to have extra funds. These funds , if they were available, are needed to take part in activities such as attending puppet shows, concerts, special classes or field trips to the zoo, for example. The public library gives families a chance to get involved in these activities no matter what their financial standings. Public library cards can be obtained by the vast majority of people. These cards provide them with access to materials they cannot normally afford to purchase. Every person may use the library's materials in house even without a card.

## WHEN TO START

"Start early for an early start" may have a familiar ring to it but some people find that it is easier said than done. Head start has begun serving children age zero and up together with their families. Many of these parents have not had experience with healthy parenting role models let alone role models to help them promote literacy in the home. This is where the library and librarian can fit in. By supplying quality materials, simple directions and examples, the librarian can empower the parent to take the first step. It does not matter what kind of family is being described, every family faces daily stress. Parents are often so busy keeping things under control in their lives, with so many things to think of and do, they often forget the simple things that mean so much to children—touching them, talking and responding to them, sharing time with them, and just being with them. The library and librarian can create an oasis for the family in its environment and programming where these things are a priority and the adult can practice needed skills.

Today we have all become aware of such terms as "quality time," "family literacy," the "hurried child" and "supertot." Much study has been placed on when to introduce literature to children. When a child enters the first grade he or she is not automatically ready to read. They have been practicing reading readiness skills long before they enter school. They have been listening, observing, imitating, practicing all in preparation for literacy or the ability to read and write one's own native language. This is important not only for success in school and work, but to survive in the world today. Children need to have the following:

1. printed material around them,
2. an adult who reads aloud to the child as well as to his or herself,
3. availability of paper, pencil or other writing material, and
4. an adult who responds to the child's questions and attempts at reading.

The most important connection between literacy/literature and the child is a caring adult who will actively participate with the child in exploring the world of language. Without a book-loving role model the book or printed matter is no more than a toy for the child to play with, and then discard when it is no longer of interest.

This is not a new area that has just come under examination by the library community. Some libraries in the United States have been running programs for infants and one year olds since the 1970's. A variety of these programs were presented at the 1987 American Library Association preconference "Ring Around Reading," one note seemed to ring louder than some of the others. No matter what program was presented, the emphasis was not to teach the child how to read or even develop reading skills but to encourage the love of language, in all its forms, to grow within the child's experience. Creating interaction between the parent, the child, and the book was the goal of the librarians active in this area of library service to little ones.

The Lapsit program I have developed also has a specific purpose. It is not to teach children how to read, how to hold a book, nor is it intended to entertain the child and adult. My purpose is to introduce language, literature, and the library to parents and children in a positive fun manner. In doing so, this program helps parents realize what the library can offer in the way of services and materials and how we as librarians can help them succeed as parents. If you encourage families with very young children to use the library, its materials, and services at the children's earliest stages of being, you will encourage the family to develop into lifelong library users.

How can the librarian today face the increasing demands for this service with his or her own limited training, experience and resources? Why should a Lapsit program or service to the very young be offered at the public library? An even better question might be *how*? This text will supply you with the resources, program outlines and materials to give you the confidence to start meeting the needs of your community in the way you decide is best.

# 2 DO I HAVE TO?

The pressure is becoming hard to ignore. More children are entering daycare at an earlier age because of the need for two family incomes. Childcare providers are not usually trained in how to present a storytime to very young children or select material for them. Families are looking for affordable activities to do together when family time is at a premium. Poverty and inner city life challenges the family structure. News stories of all types of abuse are prevalent in the daily papers nation wide. Teenagers are assuming the role of adult/parent before they even know who they are. At the opposite end of the scale some adults are becoming first time parents later in life after they have become established in their careers. This group may find it challenging to relax into the parent role, wanting to be the "super-parent" and be self conscious of everything they do with the child. Immigrants *also* face challenges with English being their second language, something that many find difficult to conquer.

Family literacy is being promoted by national organizations like the American Library Association, Head Start, educators and the government. Former First Lady, Barbara Bush, has continued to promote reading as a way to increase family literacy and togetherness. Today's jobs demand higher education and those who do not read often do not succeed. Many families find themselves trapped in a vicious cycle that is difficult to escape from no matter where they fall in the American society.

## WHAT CAN WE DO?

What can be done and does the library really have to do anything? There is much that can be done and some libraries are already doing it by reaching towards their goals. The inquiries for storytimes, programs and services for infants and children under the age of two are increasing. Libraries are expanding their goals to serve the very young child and their caregivers. Book publishers are putting more investment into materials for the very young child. Board books, a popular item for children who are still exploring the world with their mouths, have been increasing in quality, the quantity of titles available, and unfortunately price. Providing materials and programs that meet the recreational and educational need of their library's community is also a way of serving the family. In the midst of all this is the children's librarian feeling the stress to create more diversified programs, expand outreach, maintain collection development work, with an often shrinking budget and improve their reader's advisory skills. What in the world can a librarian do? Start at the beginning and start simple.

## THINGS TO THINK ABOUT FIRST

First examine your community to see if this is a needed area of service. Is there a community college that offers a program of parent education that includes children and adults. Perhaps a hospital has a program for new parents and children to attend together. The park and recreation for your city and county may already have programs for this clientele. Don't forget private and public daycare and learning facilities and other agencies such as the Red Cross or school district.

- Are there waiting lists for these programs and services and how long are they?
- Are these programs for parent education, a planned activity time for parents and children to interact together or simply a visiting time for getting together by families?

Examine your own resources to see what you have already available in-house. It could be a simple pathfinder helping adults to find materials in the library on their own or a special parenting area set up to provide easy access to materials related to parenting. Creating booklists of suggested titles for parents and children in this age group can be developed or expanded upon and made available for easy patron access. There are reference books that parents would find useful if they were aware they existed. These materials can be found through the catalog with subject searches. A card file of general topics that parents inquire about can also be created and may be used more by adults who often "have a child in tow". General topics—for example, general parenting skills, child development, arts and crafts, discipline, etc.—can be used to organize the file and enable the parent to locate materials he or she needs or wants. A card file tends to be more specific than a pathfinder. It can be browsed through by the patron without the librarian's direct assistance and is not that difficult to keep current. Basic bibliography and call numbers are necessary information for these cards; annotations are useful but not mandatory. Compiling a directory of childcare facilities, daycares, and programs available for this age group also enables the librarian to meet the needs of this clientele when facing limited resources. These materials could be housed in a special area known as "the parenting area" to enable easy access. If space is limited a shelf or bulletin board could be designated for that purpose.

The next things to take into consideration are when to offer this program or service and how often. Enthusiasm by patrons and librarians indicates that every week would be the best of all possible situations. Take into consideration that this program initially needs time to prepare for and energy to conduct, often more than that of a preschool storytime. To keep the materials fresh and the program on a quality level, pace yourself. The following options are available:

1. a series of programs lasting a certain number of weeks,
2. offer programs seasonally,
3. offer the class once a month perhaps in conjunction with libraries in your surrounding area, and
4. present program(s) during a special month devoted to parenting or families.

Be careful not to overbook yourself. Remember, this program is supposed to serve as an introduction for the child and parent or family caregiver to the world of literature and libraries.

## STAFFING

Staff restrictions also need to be considered in the areas of training and scheduling. Self-education must be done prior to the program to ensure adequate behavior awareness and proper selection of materials by the librarian. This can be accomplished through reading and research by the librarian, or by attending workshops and classes in other facilities. If it is possible, the interested librarian should observe another presenter running this kind of program. Doing this has proven to be beneficial for librarians. It may also be possible to arrange an exchange program with other librarians who have run these programs before by offering to conduct a program of yours for their library. Hiring an expert in child development or parenting and limiting the literacy portion of the program is also an option. (See Chapter 5 for various program formats.) However, this program does demand the librarian' full attention. This means that they will not be available for reference services in the library during this time period. If there is a limited number of librarians on staff, maybe this program could be scheduled before the library opens. Selecting an evening when there is more than one librarian scheduled or a low reference demand is another possibility. Programs can also be conducted on Saturday mornings, but often this is the time when families prefer to stay at home.

## ADVERTISING YOUR PROGRAMS

How do you let the public know you are offering programs for this very young age group? Keep it brief and simple. In King County we extend an invitation directed at the adult to explore the wonderful world of language with their child using simple stories, fingergames, songs, and rhymes. State clearly that this program is designed for very young children and adults together. Siblings are not encouraged to enable one to one ratio during this program. This program requires nurturing at the start because the library has not been the location for this age groups' activities. Try sending publicity to places like the local hospitals and health clinics. Some areas have parent support groups or newsletters where this information can be included. Check for special newspapers that target parents of very young children. Be careful when choosing graphics and avoid stereotypes whenever possible. We once received a picture of a woman wearing an apron playing with an infant, but the target audience was working parents with children ages 12 to 24 months, so the graphic was inappropriate and was replaced. From that time a picture of a male sharing a book with a young child has been our Lapsit graphic with great success.

## PREPARATION AND MATERIALS

Preparation and materials are an essential part of this program and these too can be simplified. By using a core set of materials the librarian can repeat basically the same program and keep it interesting by varying fingergames and other incidentals Children of this age group often have favorite stories and rhymes that can be used for every program. The children gain recognition skills in knowing a story when the title is mentioned, parents memories are refreshed with old and familiar tales and rhymes, and the librarian has a program ready to go with a few embellishments.

# WHY SHOULD I?

"There are no little ones in my library." This statement is a two-edged sword. The old image of the library being a quiet study haven has basically been revamped, and hopefully children of all ages are welcome. Do not assume that is a fact until you have looked carefully at your library first.

Is the children's area safe and comfortable place for small people and does it encourage adults to stay and browse through the books with their child? The atmosphere of the children's area can be changed drastically by adding simple items. For example, a bright rug to designate the children's area, a storage for board books (place in a plastic crate instead of shelves), a rocking chair to cuddle in or bright posters on the walls can create a friendly feeling to the area. Displays of books, booklists, and pathfinders in an area where they can be accessible also encourage adults to use the library and its materials. Check for electrical outlets that should be covered to prevent children from examining them too closely and getting hurt.

Some patrons, when asked why they don't bring their child to the library or think of going to the library with their child, respond that they feel uncomfortable and unwelcome in the library environment. One parent stated that the librarian complained to her about her child who was being fussy that day. These perceptions should be of great concern to us, because the comment cited here was made by a teen mother. Librarians are so involved with other areas of service or unsure of how to help this age group, we often forget that a simple "Hello, may I help you" or "Someone is having a fussy day. Need any help?" will put the patron with an active little one at ease.

The variety of services to choose from are not limited to programs alone. The patrons who participate in the library's programs and avail themselves of its services respond, for the most part, with enthusiasm and often amazement. Family literacy is encouraged when adults read aloud to their children and the adult's own reading skills can be improved with the practice. Adults forget or may not be aware of how many skills must first be developed by the child before reading can begin. By using simple explanations and examples the librarian can empower the adult to welcome their child to the world of language and develop communication.

# BENEFITS

Finally, in response to "why", here are some benefits of programming and serving the very young child and his or her caregiver along with comments from actual participants of Lapsit programs:

1. The librarian role models how to share stories, fingergames, songs and interact with the very young child. The librarian can reassure the adults that each child is unique and will participate when ready and to the degree that he or she is able to. By use of repetition and demonstration the librarian also demonstrates how children learn. They can set the adult at ease with a relaxed performance.

*"My child has spontaneously initiated some of the rhyming songs with me. She remembered!"*

2. Selecting age appropriate materials and materials of interest to the adult, the librarian can help create awareness of the vast variety of books, media, and resources the adult may not be aware of but would find useful. It helps minimize the frustration of non-library users trying to locate material they are looking for.

*"Through the librarian, we discovered and (had) brought to our attention wonderful books and tapes, etc. that we would have spent months finding on our own!"*

*"The class taught me to choose more appropriate books-also the class was fun!"*

3. The primary "rule" in serving this age group is to actively involve the adults during the program and give them the confidence that they are doing a good job. With the increase of working parents, programs such as Lapsit helps create a special time where the adult can interact and concentrate on their very young child. This is good for single parents, working parents and for the adult who may not be the primary caregiver but desired that "quality time" with their child.

*"As a working father, I appreciated the opportunity to see my son interact with other children. Gave us a specific date and time where I would be dedicating time only to him not distracted by our older children and their homework, etc. My son wasn't too interested in the activities at first. Each week he spent more time participating."*

*(Lapsit) "was something my child and I learned together."*

4. The librarian can help the adult recreate this sharing experience on their own and promote family literacy.

*"The fun the children had and the ease with which creative Lapsit ideas were transferred to home activities."*

5. This program and variations of it can be used to reach non-library users in their environment—for example, alternate high schools, Head Start programs, shelters and even daycares. It can promote the library as a place not only of books but of fun and resources.

*"My child now thinks its a great treat to go to the library."*

*"I never realized how much the library had that much stuff I'd be interested in and I never thought of it as a place to take my 14 month old. I know better now!"*

6. It is true that the earlier the child is exposed to language and literature the more likely that he or she will gain the skills necessary for literacy. Adults may not have the resources or materials available to them. They may not even have experienced this type of program and not realize its importance. The library can enlighten them and empower them with its services and programs in this area.

7. By setting an example, the librarian can help the adult learn how to share literature with their child and practice it in a positive manner. Using vocal expression, demonstrating how to play fingergames, and mixing up words helps adults become comfortable in the world of words with their children.

8. When the Lapsit program is familiar it can be adapted to various forms and used for presentations in non library settings.

A number of librarians have found Lapsit to be an experience that has returned much more than their initial investment of time and resources. The program has proven to be versatile, flexible, and rewarding. I have discovered that many of the families that participated have become regular library users after the completion of the Lapsit Program.

Lapsit has also been used successfully with teen parents. It has been useful in instructing them how to communicate and interact with their children. It has enabled them to better utilize libraries and their services while gaining confidence in their parenting skills. "Super-parents" are given the permission to relax and enjoy the language experience with their children and be less than perfect.

Materials and resources are given to the people who need and would benefit from them the most. The library is no longer thought of as "just a place with lots of books." It is an interested, actively involved part of the family's daily life with people, materials, resources, and services at their disposal.

# 3 WHAT CAN I DO?

Don't limit yourself into thinking that you can only serve children in this age group and their caregivers by developing programs in the library or that the librarian always has to be the presenter. The variety of programs and services are as numerous as there are librarians willing to conduct them. The programs can be aimed at the adult or caregiver, with or without the child. Services can be provided by the library or the library can serve as the resource for other community agencies. The presenter can be the local librarian or someone from the outside community who has training.

Programs and services for this age group and their caregivers can be divided into two basic areas. The first is outreach—library programs and services that are offered by the library at sites outside of the library. The second is in-house—materials, programs, and services that can be provided by the librarian and library within its own domain. Books and other materials borrowed from the library are used in many child-service agencies as well as in homes without the involvement of librarians.

## OUTREACH

Outreach is an important way of serving this patron group. The target audience is a busy one with the adult involved in day to day activities and often under great stress in coping with the basics of living, and often unaware of the child's need to learn. The library is usually one of the last places young parents would think about going to for fun. They also tend to be non-library users because they have been away from the library environment and its services, or are people with less education and less economic security and are unaware of how they can take advantage of even basic library services.

Reaching out to do programming such as Lapsit in the community can provide increased awareness of library services and materials available to the public. It also focuses the attention on a contact person for child and family-serving agencies, associations, or individuals to call upon. By offering programs at sites frequently visited by a young parent, the librarian encourages venturing into the world of language and libraries.

Outreach services can take place in connection with hospitals, parent support groups, community colleges, and day care providers. The scope of the outreach must be determined by each library, its planning based on a thorough knowledge of the resources needed. For example, alternative high schools for teenage parents, Head

Start groups and even pediatricians can benefit by exposure to the library, its materials, and services.

Begin by compiling a mailing list using the local phone book, local directories, community resource files, and even licensing agencies. Start with what is presently manageable and expand as you are able to overcome limitations. Before offering materials and services make sure you will be able to meet the demand.

## OUTREACH USING PRINTED MATERIAL

One of the preliminaries in offering outreach services is a letter of introduction by the librarian reminding the groups of the library resources available to them, its hours, location, general services and a contact persons name with a phone number. Library non-users may need to be invited; remind the public library is there for them and told of the improvements that may have taken place from the last time they last ventured through the doors. Renewing materials by phone, a quick reference answer phone number, or requesting materials by phone could be of vast interest to adults who find it difficult to leave the house with an exuberant child. Some associations may even be willing to post that information or display materials the library offers. For example, multiple copies of booklists on parenting skills, how to read to children brochures, or children's booklists for the very young child could be made available to their clientele. Hospitals, pediatricians, and daycares are only a few of the places that might be willing to display library brochures and handouts.

Newsletters compiled by the library, that focus on the very young child are also useful. These can be published monthly or quarterly on a simple sheet on both sides or printed professionally. For example, by using the topic of "spring," you could create a newsletter that includes books about spring for the adult and child to share, suggested places to go together, how to share nature with a child, rhymes and fingergames about spring, and picture book titles that pertain to springtime. Other topics that can be covered by this kind of publication include:

- Book titles for the very young child.
- Reasons why it is important to read to your child.
- Fingergames and fingergame resources.
- How to select books for the very young child.
- Tidbits of information about authors.
- Recordings- new, classic, performers-Tapes/records/compact disks
- How to use various types of media with this age group.
- Seasonal titles for children and adults to enjoy together.

- Upcoming programs that would be of interest for this group.
- Authors to know about.
- How to instill the love of language, beginning with infants.

Remember to also include the basics with this material. This would include your library's name, address, phone number, and the name of the children's librarian when possible. Newsletters enable the community to be informed about the library and its resources even if it is difficult for the librarian to be active outside of the library. These newsletters may need to be bulk mailed, or a more cost effective method of distribution needs to be set up.

Special publications can be developed with the use of grants and can involve multiple libraries as well as other associations. Baby Talk was created in 1986 by the Decatur, Illinois libraries, hospitals, and schools, funded by a federal grant. It was aimed at parents of newborns to encourage the early and continuing nurturing of the child. By supplying helpful parenting information, making the parent aware of library materials, services, and resources available, and supplying educational information, parents were helped to develop the child's attitudes and abilities from the very beginning. *"Catch Them in the Cradle"* was developed by the Orange County Library System in Orlando, Florida with a grant from the Children's Book Council. Although both of these programs are aimed at infants, they contain materials that can be used for the pretoddler or 12 to 24 month old child. In fact, Baby Talk briefly discusses Lapsit and the Illinois libraries' variation of this in-house program. These booklets were widely distributed outside of the library as a form of outreach to encourage adults to bring their children to the library.

The special publications can also be simplified and aimed primarily at the pretoddler. One program could feature a growth chart that includes more information than simple numbers on a fold-out measuring stick relating to the pre-toddler years of 12 to 24 months old. You could include recommended reading titles, developmental stages and behavior characteristics for the child recorded on the growth chart as well as tips on how to read to the very young child, when to read to them, how to hold the book, and how accentuate the voice.

## OUTREACH PRESENTATIONS

Like the programs for storytelling, songs, and modeling for parents, the final outreach examined here also involves the librarian physically outside the library. These are usually one-time events that do not demand extensive preparation but create greater visibility for the library and awareness of the scope of its services.

Participating in what has become known as "fairs" has become a method of increasing the community's awareness of libraries and the vast age range that can take advantage of its materials and resources. These can be educational fairs where schools, literacy groups, and other educational associations display their materials or fun fairs, kindergarten preparedness meetings, literacy fairs, children's activity day or parent/teacher association meetings. By distributing selected handout materials, you can show adults the variety of library materials available to them. These could include materials for the very young child—for example, board books—materials adults can use for themselves—for example, on topics like going back to work, understanding the strong-willed child, booklists of wonderful stories to share together, and services the library is eager to offer them. Extending a welcoming hand to the patrons outside of the library it is more likely that the non-library users and their families will venture into the library.

Outreach services are the most effective way in which the librarian can find and touch the life of the very young child and whose parent or caregiver. Many parents or caregivers never seek library resources or programs on their own. Outreach programs are also a way of raising the awareness of the community to the fact that librarians exist to serve all people of all ages, economic, and educational levels. The library will back up outreach efforts by developing materials and services so that when patrons do come to the library, they are not disappointed.

# IN-HOUSE MATERIALS AND SERVICES

## PRINTED MATERIALS

Publications may consist of booklists, pathfinders, activity sheets, publicity flyers, and information sheets. These can be created by the local librarian, put together by a library system, multiple librarians, or purchased from various sources.

Topics that booklists can cover include the following:

1. Recommended titles for the pretoddler.
2. Selected titles of different types of books such as board books, concept books, pop-up books, etc.
3. Recommended media for children and how to use them with children including tapes, recordings, videos, and compact disks.
4. Parenting skills and concerns—general as well as those related to learning and language.

5. Activity books for adults to use when interacting with children. For example, craft books, music books, indoor and outdoor game books.
6. Titles to help the adult who works with children on topics like fingergames, puppets, music, safety, etc.

Handouts can also be just as varied as the booklists. They can include:

1. Reasons to read to your child and when to begin.
2. Fingergames and how to do them. This may include additional resources in which to find more fingergames in books and recordings.
3. How to share literature with the very young child.
4. Programs available for this age group.
5. How to evaluate and select toys for your child.
6. Various topics such as discipline tips, safety awareness and how to select a childcare/play group for your child.

There are numerous ways to obtain booklists and handouts. Librarians can exchange their material with other librarians. This can be done locally or include a wider network of resources. Conventions are held state-wide and nationally for educators, librarians, and care providers. These often have an exchange table for attendees to "swap and shop" among themselves. These materials can be checked against the library's holdings with adjustments being made prior to duplicating. If funding is available, it is possible to purchase ready-made professional booklists and handouts from associations like the American Library Association, Children's Book Council, RIF (Reading Is Fundamental), and the National Association for the Education of Young Children. Catalogs of their materials can be obtained by writing or calling the association.

**American Library Association**
(ask to be connected with the Association for Library Service to Children)
50 East Huron Street
Chicago, Illinois 60611
phone: (800) 545-2433
fax: (312) 944-2641

**Children's Book Council**
568 Broadway
New York, New York 10012
phone: (212) 966-1990
fax: (212) 966-2073

**Reading Is Fundamental (RIF)**
600 Maryland Avenue. SW, Suite 500
Washington, DC 20024
fax: (202) 287-3196

**National Association for the Education of Young Children**
1509 16th Street NW
Washington, DC 20036
phone: (202) 232-8777
fax: (202) 328-1846

Pathfinders that enable adults to locate material that would be of use not only for themselves but their child are welcome materials to find in the library. A floor map of the library with designated areas marked on it can help the patron locate materials too. The pathfinder should include the call number area for books which cover the topics adults often request, as follows:

- parenting books,
- materials on potty training,
- crafts books,
- party/game books,
- dealing with feelings or death,
- discipline,
- special collections they should know
- reader's advisory materials for children's books,
- children's books,
- board books,
- audio tapes,
- videos and
- any other areas you want them to be aware of.

## PHYSICAL ENVIRONMENT

Creating an area in the library which welcomes the very young child with its physical arrangement and decor is essential to this group as well. These arrangements can be elaborate or simple depending on the individual library. However, it is important to always create a child safe environment.

Some libraries have been able to create children's areas that were specifically designed with the child in mind—for example, seating, shelf height, and colors used. Special features may have been added such as aquariums or a reading boat. Two examples of special designing for children are the Middle Country Public Library in Centereach, New York, and the Bellevue Regional Branch of the King County Library System in Bellevue, Washington. Both clearly had children in mind during their planning stages for it shows in their final product—different children's areas that work.

## The Middle Country Public Library

The Middle Country Public Library in New York has a program designed for the parent and the very young child in an area that is specifically designed for this age group. The area has three sections to it:

1. A resource area for adult information with library materials to check out such as books, puzzles, records and free handouts;
2. A toy and play area which is the largest section, and where most of the child/adult interaction takes place; and
3. A craft and activity area that contains many variety of toys, puppets, media, and gross motor equipment all on low shelves for easy access. The activity area has easy craft instructions with materials for the adult and the child to do together.

All areas are clearly indicated with signs and bright colors. It is a welcoming place for everyone who participates and made as safe as possible.

*Running A Parent/Child Workshop: A How-To-Do-It Manual for Librarians,* by Sandra Feinberg and Kathleen Deerr (Neal-Schuman Publishers, 1995), goes into great detail on how to develop a parent/child workshop that makes the best use of this space. The text includes room design, setting up and running the workshop, forms used, costs involved, and detailed appendices on materials used, resources for the materials, handouts, and bibliographies

## The Bellevue Regional Library

The Bellevue Regional Library of the King County Library System has a children's area that needed to serve a wider range of ages and still create an atmosphere welcoming the adult and very young child. By incorporating low shelving, chairs and tables built on a child-size scale and easy access to board books and puppets they have succeeded. The children are not overwhelmed by an adult size area where they cannot find materials or feel comfortable. There are also cushioned benches built into some of the bookshelves and benches that are located near windows that encourage the adult and child to cuddle and share a storybook. The area has a castle motif, flags, and boldly uses primary colors that draw the child and adult into a world of books they can enjoy together. A separate storytime room is located in the children's area and it has a special child-size doorway just for children to use which enhances the enjoyment of their storytime experience.

Libraries that are more limited in space and funding may need to simplify when they are creating or enhancing their children's space for the very young child but it can still be accomplished. A bright colored rug, a rocking chair, comfortable seating that encourages the adult and child to curl up together and share a story, easy access to board books, the use of spine indicators or markers to help make books for this age group easy to locate and a smile to welcome all, serve to create an atmosphere indicating that the library and its staff wants them to enjoy their visit.

Safety is very important and should be a high priority when serving this age group. Inspect the area for uncovered electrical outlets, loose wires that encourage tugging, items that might be pulled off by curious hands such as heavy books on display and floors cleared of potentially harmful objects—for example, staples, tacks, scissors, etc.

By creating a welcoming and safe environment for the very young child the librarian encourages the accompanying adult to relax and share the library and its materials with their child.

Additional in-house services can include the following:

1. A special section for parenting books and materials. This can be a whole unit of shelves or one shelf. If space is limited a sign indicating areas would also work. You may want to use a portable book rack that would enable you to display a few books or highlight many at one time.

2. A notebook that contains copies of booklists to help the adult locate materials when the librarian is unavailable. This can be created by using a three-ring binder with plastic page protectors. Insert the booklist into the page protector, and then place in the binder. Use oversized dividers to arrange booklists by subjects. Parenting and the very young child could be topics you can indicate.

3. Create a folder or notebook that has daycare or child care provider information. Include information booklets about how to select a child care/preschool, how to form a playgroup, and information about agencies in the area. Many libraries post flyers from daycares and preschools on a community bulletin board. This folder/notebook would enable the adult to locate all the information, in one place, about available agencies.

4. Finally, an in-house service that should not be ignored is that of reader's advisory. The librarian needs to be familiar with the styles and types of books that appeal to very young children. Awareness of reference materials to aid the adult in locating materials is also important. The *New Read-Aloud Handbook, Second*

*Edition* by Jim Trelease (Viking Penguin, 1989) includes titles for the very young child. *Choosing Books For Kids: Choosing The Right Book For The Right Child At The Right Time,* by Joanne Oppenheim, Barbara Brenner and Betty Boegehold (Ballantine Trade, 1986) is also informative. Be aware that in these resources, the latest titles are often not included. One of the newer resource books is *Mother Goose Comes First: An Annotated Guide To The Best Books and Recordings For Your Preschool Child* by Lois Winkel and Sue Kimmel (Henry Holt & CO., 1990). Although this is aimed at the preschool child the sections on Mother Goose, lullabies, and concept books can be applied to the very young child; it also contains some newer titles in addition to classics.

## REFERENCE BOOKS:

*A to Zoo: Subject Access to Children's Picture Books.* Carolyn W. Lima and John A. Lima. Fourth edition. New Jersey R.R. Bowker, 1993.

*American Library Association Best of the Best for Children: books, magazines, videos, audio, software, toys, travel.* Denise Perry Donavin, Ed. New York: Random House, 1992.

*Choosing Books for Kids: Choosing the Right Book for the Right Child at the Right Time.* Joanne Oppenheim, Barbara Brenner and Betty Boegehold. New York: Ballantine Books, 1986.

*Mother Goose Comes First: An Annotated Guide to the Best Books and Recordings for Your Preschool Child.* Lois Winkel and Sue Kimmel. New York: Henry Holt and Company, 1990.

*Play, Learn and Grow: an Annotated Guide to the Best Books and Materials for Very Young Children.* James L. Thomas. New Jersey: R.R. Bowker, 1992.

*The New Read-Aloud Handbook, 2nd ed.* Jim Trelease. New York: Penguin Books, 1989.

## PROGRAMS FOR ADULTS: PARENTS AND CARERGIVERS

Programs that can be conducted in-house or as outreach are useful to have prepared, and because they are usually attended by adults only they can be classified as adult education programs. Some librarians may also feel more comfortable doing a presentation without the children present. These serve a multitude of groups because they can be designed for the specific group to which it is being presented. Materials for all of the programs remain basic with additional materials being selected to specialize it for the group.

The basic core of the program is the librarian's talk about the importance of reading and communicating with children in addition to the services and materials provided by the library. Materials could include library location and hours, library card applications, flyers of library programs, and booklists the audience would find informative. Special books to bring to their attention could be parenting books, board books, or any other special materials you have for the very young child. In the case of care providers, promote books that encourage language and literature between the adult and very young child.

When exploring the realm of adult education programs, expand your horizons to encompass other professions such as those in the health and education field. Promoting reading aloud, sharing rhymes, and discovering the world of language with the very young child is as important for health and child care professionals to know about as it is for parents.

Other groups that would benefit from an adult education program that promotes reading to the very young child can be found in colleges that have early education studies, licensing training for care providers, high schools, alternative schools for teens, English as a Second Language classes, and even park district staffs.

As stated, some librarians may prefer to interact with adults rather than with the child. Adult education programs can inform the adult of the basic reasons why it is important to begin communicating with the child at the earliest possible time and supplies the adult with the basic tools and skills for doing this successfully. It is useful at times to include audio-visual material along with your booktalk and presentation. An excellent video to incorporate into an adult education program that covers the very young child is *Read To Me: Libraries, Books and Your Baby,* produced by the greater Vancouver Library Federation. It is a fifteen minute program that demonstrates the following:

1. stresses the importance of reading to babies to help develop their language skills,
2. shows the variety of library services a community library offers, and
3. states that teaching is a natural part of parents and other caregivers responsibilities.

The video has a range of children in it from infants to early walkers.

# PROGRAMS FOR THE CHILD AND ADULT

Some of the most effective and exciting programs are the ones which involve both the child and the adult. For purpose of division and simplicity we will in this text describe these age groups in the following manner:

| | |
|---|---|
| Infant | birth to 12 months. |
| Pretoddler | 12 months to 24 months. |
| Toddler | 24 months to 36 months. |
| Preschooler | ages 3 years to 5 years. |
| Adult | The parent or caregiver who attends the program with the child. |

Programs can be planned with a session for each of these age groups as a stand-alone offering or as a series. Adults attend with the child at least until the preschool level, and then it is up to the librarian's discretion if the adult is required to attend. Because much has been written about toddler and preschool programs we are focusing this book on programs for the infant and pretoddler. Before exploring the programs let us first understand the participants.

# BUILDING BRIDGES

Thoughtful leaders in business and government as well as in the arts and education fields are in agreement with librarians that reading needs to be a vital part of everyone's daily life. Reading aloud has no limitations as to who reads to whom or how old someone has to be in order to enjoy listening to a story. The public library is a reading resource for everyone. Why is it then that relatively few public libraries offer programming for children under the age of 18 months? Judith Dixon and Frances Smardo Dowd report in a national survey of children's coordinators about programs for babies in the public library (Public Libraries, Jan/Feb, 1993, page. 29). To the initial question of

> "Does your library, or do any of your branch libraries, regularly offer literature-related programming (such as storytime or "lap-sits") specifically for children under the age of eighteen months?"

The majority of 74 percent said no. That means of the 119 that responded to the survey only 31 had regular programming for the very young child and 88 did not. Why is it that there are so few libraries serving the development needs of this age group? The reason cited most by libraries that do not have regularly scheduled programs for very young children is the staff lacks training and expertise. More libraries would attempt serving this age group if there were additional knowledgeable employees or educated volunteers available.

How does a librarian begin to build the bridges that connect the caring adult, the very young child, and literature/library together? Having a basic understanding of each of the participants may be the best way to start.

## THE INFANT

Librarians have expressed concern about running programs where the child, in this case the infant, does not actively participate. They tend to see this as simply an adult education program. For the most part this is true however, the child is participating in a way that is not often understood by the librarian. Infants learn about the world around them by using their senses. They are aware of sounds, touch, taste and sight. They have a very limited way of communicating through their cries and coos. What can the librarian do with children who have no basic foundation of language skills and literature? Get them started! How? By enabling the adult to build a bridge of language and communication with his or her child.

Infants need to find out about the world and themselves. What better way then through rhythm and rhyme? Body awareness can be accomplished by using such rhymes as "Head and Shoulders, Knees and Toes." Including the child's name in such rhymes as the following adds a personal touch to the rhyme.

"These are *(child's name)* fingers, these are *(child's name)* toes, this is *(child's name)* bellybutton, round and round it goes!".

Fingergames, songs, and poetry are very important because infants respond to the beat that is reminiscent of the heartbeat they heard in the womb. Repetition is the way to build familiarity that will create anticipation in the child for what is to come when the fingergame, song, or poem is heard. Children's learning begins when they start to develop their listening skills. Children's listening skills come before comprehension skills in the learning process, followed by vocalization. Dr. Jerry Paul stated at the American Library Association's pre-conference in 1987 that "gaze plus movement plus vocalization equals communication." The interaction between the child, book, and adult taken at the child's pace enables him or her to experience the book and world around them. Vocally the librarian can demonstrate how to read stories, poems, and songs to help the adult gain confidence exploring the world of language with the child. They can verify that infants make no judgment of the adults abilities but adore them for whatever they share with the child. If the adult is self conscious about his or her vocal abilities, the librarian can recommend quality tapes that are not only useful at home but in the car tape player as well. Children are often calmed by familiar melodies or rhymes that help them refocus when the outside world overwhelms them with its sounds and stimulation.

Naomi Baron, in her book *Growing Up With Language: How Children Learn to Talk,* explains the four essential language components this way:

> "The smallest building blocks of language are sounds (that is, consonants and vowels, liquids and glides)that can be combined to make up words. Words individually have meaning, as do the phrases and sentences speakers construct using the rules of grammar. Speakers draw upon sounds, meanings and grammar to construct conversations with each other." (Page 9)

The librarian can lead the adult and child into the wonderful world of conversation/communications/language by involving them both in storytime. Sounds are discovered in poetry, songs, and rhymes. Meaning is discovered from repetition and association as in the case of tickle rhymes and fingergames. Grammar comes into play with sharing picture books that involve simple sentences and simple stories. All three—sounds, meaning, and structure—build communication between the adult and child. The child's love of sounds can blossom into love of language and literature that can be shared with a caring adult. Jim Trelease states "If a child is old enough to talk to, he's old enough to be read to." (*New Read-Aloud Handbook,* pg. 20) The librarian's responsibility is to enlarge the adult's primary image of a book to include poetry, songs, newspapers, shopping lists, rhymes, and other items that language is a major part. By demonstrating what fun this experience can be and the necessity for a good foundation early in life the librarian can bring the infant and adult into the world of language and literature.

For more information about infants here are additional resources:

Ames, Louise Bates, Ph.D., Frances L Ilg, MD, and Carol Chase Haber. *Your One Year Old: the fun loving fussy 12 to 24 month old.* New York: Dell Publishing, 1982.

Miller, Karen. *Ages and Stages: Developmental descriptions and activities birth through eight years.* Telshare Publishing Company, Inc., 1985.

White, Burton L. *The First Three Years of Life.* Revised edition. Englewood Cliffs, NJ: Prentice-Hall, 1987.

## THE PRETODDLER

In order to work with children between the ages of 12 and 24 months, or as we shall call them "pretoddlers," one needs a basic understanding of their development and behavior patterns. The child is in-between the total dependency on adults of an infant and the toddler who demands independence. Starting to venture off on their own they begin to explore the world around them making sure their anchor (primary caretaker) is close at hand. They are still shy and leery of venturing too far into the "unknown." Manipulating, conquering, and learning about the physical world around him or her, the pretoddler is gaining confidence in a world of simple motion and action. Physical skills demand their concentration with large motor skills being mastered first. They are discovering their mobility and go through each day exuding the thrill of being alive.

Things begin to change for the child between the ages of 13 and 18 months. The child's thinking mind begins to emerge with symbols, images, and concepts being added to the physical world awareness around them. A sense of self comes into being and the children begin to realize they are separate individuals—a person! There is a wide variation in how children deal with becoming individuals and each moves at his or her own pace. The young pretoddler is concerned for the most part with mastering the large motor skills such as walking, throwing and catching a ball, walking up and down stairs, sitting and standing. Fine motor skills include the grasping of thumb and forefinger, scribbling, dumping small items from a container and turning the pages of a book two or three at a time. Intellectually, the young pretoddler can follow simple directions like "stop," use names of familiar objects, and understand more than can be verbally expressed. In regard to language development at this age, the child uses body gestures to express themselves rather than verbalizing. They can identify parts of their body, familiar people, animals and objects when asked to, and they can imitate familiar words. Their comprehension is much greater than their verbalizing. Their attention span is short—one to two minutes. Pretoddlers love to imitate the world around them and when they are not actively mimicking it, they are observing it.

The older pretoddler, ages 18 to 24 months, has begun to master these physical skills and starts to concentrate on other areas such as the development of speech and language. It often proves to be a frustrating time for children who are not quite able to verbalize what they feel and are still learning how to deal with being a separate individual. Mastering the skills of simple communication and speech helps pretoddlers deal with their world. The pretoddler's abilities to use large motor skills continues to grow. They can jump in place with two feet together, stairs are becoming less of an obstacle, and arms and legs can be individually lifted up high. Fine motor skills are also being developed—pages of a book can be turned one at a time, objects can be rotated and put into openings such as puzzle pieces fitting into a puzzle. Intellectually, the child remembers and retains more information. Following simple directions, naming objects when asked "What is this?", identifying simple pictures and trying to sing are a few of the skills the pretoddler works on mastering at this stage. Routine and having an order to things becomes important to the pretoddler to enhance a sense of security and growing confidence. The development of speech and language skills develops more rapidly at this age than at any other time during the pretoddler's life. Their vocabulary has grown to 15 to 20 words or more. Listening to rhymes, songs and repetition of sounds is a favorite pastime. By creating conversations with toys or with themselves the pretoddler practices the skills necessary in communicating.

With all the newfound knowledge and experiences the pretoddlers are having, they can become frustrated and overwhelmed. Recognizing when the child needs a break from the stimulus can be accomplished by "reading" their body language and vocalization. Crying, turning away, wiggling, loss of eye contact and even falling asleep indicates the child has had enough for now. Slowing down the pace or taking a break is the best way to prevent the language sharing experience from becoming something to be dreaded by the child.

Throughout this whole age range children move at their own unique pace. Each child develops at a different rate because it takes concentration to grow. For example, when concentrating on learning how to walk, the fine motor skills or language development may take a back seat for a while until the new skill is mastered. The sense of being a separate individual is still new and unfamiliar to the child. While discovering and testing their separateness pretoddlers often reach back for their familiar caregiver for reassurance and protection. They watch other children, but most do not initiate interacting with them. Separation anxiety is easily recognized in this age group but with a familiar routine, environment, and people the pretoddler will grow comfortable enough to explore and master their world.

## THE ADULT

In addition to having an understanding of the child it is also useful to have an understanding of the adult who attends the Lapsit program as well. Those adults may be first time parents, experienced parents, working parents, or teen parents. If not a parent, the adult is someone who cares about the child. No matter what their background or experience, they have one thing in common—they want the best for their children and they want to share the experience with them.

Parents today are often pulled in many directions. Working parents, teenage parents, families that are separated from one another geographically and changing social roles all impact how children are being brought up today. The stress level is often very high and parents may feel isolated from each other and society. The demands of work, the demands of childhood, the demands of self, and the demands of daily living constantly tug at the adult throughout the day. Fathers want to take a more active roll in their child's life and the working mother may feel the heavy-weight of guilt for being away from the child. Teen parents may find themselves unsure of their parenting skills with limited role models to imitate. This is often the case for older first time parents as well. Parents want to do it "*right*" and thereby create their own tension because they are unsure of what is right.

> "Our very desire to do the best for our children makes us nervous. Although we have all been children, we forget what being a child is like." (*Before the Basics* by Bev Bos, page 5).

Parents have been absorbed by the infant until now. The changes and developments of their child at this stage often overwhelms them as they strive to understand and communicate with the pretoddler. Just as the child struggles with self identity, the adult has to adjust to his or her role. As the child gains mobility so does the adult's awareness of wanting to keep the child safe and enable the child to manage the world being explored.

Parents usually strive to give their child the "best," however it is they define that term. They often become entangled with their desire to "do it right." Many times they complicate matters, creating their own difficulties. For instance, reading to their child has been promoted as vitally important to their child's learning experience. Told to read fifteen minutes a day the adult often does not realize that this time can be spread throughout the whole day. It also indicates that many things can be read such as signs, grocery lists, songs and rhymes not only books. Adults, when reminded, will realize they already know many songs, rhymes, and stories from their own childhood. They just need a refresher course of what they enjoyed as a child. The librarian can also make suggestions of various times reading can be incorporated into the family's daily life. Most adults read to their child at bedtime which creates a routine to end the day. Other times can be included in normal routines such as changing diapers or taking a walk. It is an added bonus when the adult enjoys the story, song, or rhyme, lets their enthusiasm become evident and instills in the child's consciousness that words, rhythm, and meanings—all the aspects of reading are fun.

Many things that the adult takes for granted the child may have no knowledge or experience of. Adults need to realize the child is learning about their world the only way they can—by using their senses. The physical makeup of a book is unknown to them. They have no concept at first that books have a front or back, cover or pages, or that there is a proper way to hold the book. Children do not realize paper will tear and because repetition is how they learn many pages may be put to the test. The young pretoddler may also explore a book the only way he or she knows how—by using their senses, usually their mouth. The caring adult will show by example how to hold a book, how to handle a book and experience the book with the child. Give the child have an old catalog or better still, a board or cloth book, to practice turning pages with until the book handling skills are mastered.

Talk about the book together and touch the cover and pages, demonstrating how to turn the pages. If the mouth is still the major source of exploration for the child, the adult can supply board books, cloth or vinyl books for their child's individual handling and reserve the paper books to be shared together. Creating a positive experience not only with the story but with the physical book itself enables both the child and adult to enjoy the experience.

The economy does not help relieve the stress or frustration a parent feels when confronted with financial limitations. Seeing the child chew or rip an expensive picture book does not allow positive interaction between adult and child to take place. Publishing costs may push the development of home libraries out of reach for many families. Adults need to know what materials are available at the public library and that it's use is affordable—it's free.

Some adults may be so enthusiastic about creating and sharing their literary experience with their child that they overwhelm him or her. The pace is important so the child can absorb and assimilate what is happening around him or her physically and verbally. Letting the child set the pace enables the adult and the child to share the experience together, and involves the child in the learning process to help build communication between them both.

## THE LIBRARIAN

The role of the librarian is a major component to building bridges between the child, the adult, and the literary experience. Concern has been expressed by the librarian regarding the following:

1. not having staff with the knowledge or expertise in the area of early childhood development,
2. not wanting to be just an entertainer,
3. not being sure of how to relate to a group of children who have no idea of what a book is and are constantly on the move.

One of the major drawbacks to programming in this area is that many librarians do not feel competent in their knowledge of child development especially for very young children. Children's librarians seem unaware of how well they are prepared to begin serving pretoddlers or children ages 12 to 24 months. By using songs, fingergames and stories they already know, the librarian can adapt them to the abilities of the very young child. The diversity of abilities can fluster the librarian when confronted with a group that includes children who have not discovered mobility with those who never seem to stop moving around. The librarian can reassure the adults that the earlier the language experience begins, the sooner the child grows familiar with language. Children are always learning and observing life around them even when they do not seem to be.

Yes, the older pretoddler can participate individually to a greater extent than the younger ones. It is the adult's involvement that can draw the younger pretoddler into the literature sharing experience. For example, "Hickory, Dickory Dock" is a rhyme familiar to almost everyone. The librarian can suggest that the child clasp their hands together to create a clock, the adult can hold the child if he or she is not walking yet and make them a clock or run their fingers up the child's body at the appropriate part of the rhyme. "Row, Row, Row Your Boat" can be done together with the child and adult acting out the action on the floor or in a chair.

Librarians don't need to be experts in the area of early childhood development in order to asist adults to find resources to help them better understand their child. Self education can be accomplished by reading materials on early childhood development or attending workshops often available at local hospitals or clinics. Colleges also have classes to select from if more formalized education is desired. When a question or situation occurs in the class it is useful to state that you will research that during the week and return to the next class with some conclusions regarding it. Keep a pad of paper and pencil by the display area so that the adults can jot questions on the pad along with their name and phone number. This way, confusion is kept to a minimum during the program and the question has a greater chance of being satisfactorily answered.

There are a number of useful resources available for librarians who are interested in learning more about early childhood development. *Early Childhood Literature Sharing Programs in Libraries* by Ann Carlson gives an excellent overview of childhood developments and affirm through research the high degree to which library practice is in tune with it. *Babies Need Books* by Dorothy Butler has a great deal of information that is presented in a clear, concise manner and is defiantly one that will inspire the reader to venture into this area of library service. Jim Trelease's book *The New Read-Aloud Handbook* is useful for librarians as well as other adults interested in instilling the love of reading in the very young child. *Please Touch* by Susan Striker, useful in understanding the creative development patterns for young children and in helping to reassure the adults that children develop at their own pace. There are numerous early childhood books and I recommend Louise Bates Ames book entitled *Your One-Year Old: The Fun-Loving Fussy 12 to 24 Month Old*. There are more resources available and these are listed in the suggested readings.

There are librarians who see this kind of programming for the very young child to be one of entertainment and they are the performer. To a degree this may be true, but then it is also true with preschool storytime as well. By making sure that literacy is at the root of the program the librarian is acting as a guide and educator to the world of language. This is where the love of reading is nurtured and the desire to read begins. The librarian becomes the role model for the adult on how to instill the love of reading in a child. the parent or caregiver is learning how to interact with the child by the use of fingergames, songs, rhymes, and when using a book. The adult becomes keenly aware of the literary experience the child and librarian are sharing during a enthusiastic reading of a book and they want to duplicate it for themselves at home. As one adult stated on in an evaluation, "I learned much more seeing the songs (stories, rhymes) demonstrated then I would have from a book." The child and adult gain security in knowing that the library is a place that is fun and welcomes them. This programming enables the librarian to demonstrate how to keep the literary sharing experience a positive one. By actively demonstrating how to hold a book and when to share it with the child the librarian gives the adult the ability to recreate the experience on their own. The librarian is not just an entertainer but educator and role model.

In regard to being able to interact with the child and adult, the librarian needs to keep in mind a few things. This program needs to be experienced to be fully understood. It does deserve an enthusiastic and quality presentation. If your personality or professional attitudes continue to protest after your initial venture into Lapsit programming it would be best to explore the other variety of services for this age group. If need be have an outside presenter work in conjunction with you or variation of the program may suffice, such as an adult education/booktalk presentation.

I have found adults and children to be very aware of the energy and dedication a librarian has towards this program. The key is active involvement by the librarian when doing the Lapsit program. If the children are overly active concentrate on the fingergames and action rhymes. Help the children to regroup with their caregiver if they are wandering by telling them to find Mommy, Daddy, or whomever they are with. Incorporating it into a rhyme or game can help. For example, after "Cobbler, Cobbler, mend my shoe" ask the children to find the adult and mend their shoe! When reading, use your voice to center their attention them back with the story by your expressiveness or use of animal sounds. Relax and share the literature experience with the children on their level. Make sure to have eye contact with the child, use non-threatening gestures and an enthusiastic presentation, warmed with a smile can open the doorway to Lapsit fun for everyone involved.

The librarian is the bridge builder who can help the very young child and a caring adult cross over into the exciting realm of language, literature, and communication.

# 4 LAPSIT: WHAT IS IT?

Lapsit is not a new term. I first heard it at the American Library Association pre-conference "Ring Around Reading " held in San Francisco in 1987. It was the term used to describe the San Francisco Public Library's Infant/Toddler program that had been in existence for about six years. Debby Jeffery and Ellen Mahoney also wrote about this program in their School Library Journal/April 1989 article entitled "Sitting Pretty: Infants, Toddlers and Lapsits."

Lapsit has become a familiar term at the Newport Way branch of the King County Library System in Bellevue, Washington. It is a program for 12 to 24 month old children and their caregivers (usually parents). It has been offered twice a year as a four to five week evening series since 1987. This Lapsit however, has a definition slightly different from that of San Francisco's program. Designed primarily as a storytime for very young children and adults, it also incorporates parent education and an introduction to the library and its services.

There were specific reasons for developing it this way. It seemed that children in this age group were considered too old to be infants and too young to be toddlers by many agencies in our area. Many libraries defined the age of the toddler group for storytime to be two to three years of age. Children in the pretoddler age group or those ages 12 to 24 months have discovered mobility and practice their new-found skills whenever possible. They want to move and hoping they will stay still long enough to listen to a story, even a wonderful one, seems a remote dream. Many parents avoid the library because of their child's exuberance and don't know that the library has many services offer them. Finally, as a working mother, I realized many parents were uncertain about that nebulous concept of "quality time" and how they could manage to achieve it after a busy day. An unexpected benefit came when I discovered that by changing the emphasis on the program's components they were adaptable for a variety of other programs as well. A basic program supplied a foundation that enables me to serve many age groups and do it efficiently.

## HOW TO DO IT

"How to" is often the biggest obstacle to beginning this area of library service. Because many children's librarians do not feel competent in their knowledge of child development, they hesitate to venture into another level of service unprepared. However, we are talking about professionals who have been educated for life-long learning. Through basic self-education a librarian can become familiar with the characteristics of this age group and confidently begin programming. The librarian is not the expert but a guide to the experts and resources that can be found at the library. Neither is the librarian merely a performer but rather a role model who can show by example how to use the world of language for fun and in day-to-day activities. Children's librarians seem unaware of how well they are already prepared to begin serving the pre-toddler or children ages 12 to 24 months. In Chapter 3 we examined the makeup of the child and the adult who would probably attend this kind of program. By applying this understanding to materials already in use, the librarian can adapt them to create a wonderful literature sharing experience for everyone involved.

Let's look at a specific example to illustrate. One of the areas in which the child is developing is that of large motor skills. The Eency, Weency Spider is a familiar rhyme with finger motions that many families already know. Changing it to "the Great Big Spider" and having the participants use whole arm and leg motions enables everyone to act it out. Children do not have to fumble to copy their caregiver or be frustrated in trying to follow the small finger movements. If there are prewalkers in the group, the adult can move the child's arms and legs, help them stand and move, or just carry the child as he or she is repeating the rhyme.

When reading aloud during the storytime, the librarian can set an example for the adult showing how to read stories to the child. By adding animal sounds, reading with expression, talking about the pictures or even skipping pages to shorten the story, the librarian gives the adult permission to do likewise. Many parents do not have a literary background or know how to read aloud to the child. They may not have been read to as children and feel overly self-conscious or afraid they will "not do it right." Adults often are unclear of what kind of material would be best suited for this age group. It is often possible the adult has difficulties with reading skills which could be improved with practice and reading aloud to the child. Many parents are so overwhelmed with the primary needs of day to day life that they have not thought about reading to the child. By simplifying, adapting, and looking at current resources in a new light, librarians can begin serving very young children and their caregivers.

# PROGRAM OUTLINE

## GENERAL FORMAT

The time involved in doing the Lapsit program is thirty minutes. Its best, however, to block at least an hour of time for the program session. It is best to expect families to arrive 15 minutes ahead of time and allow time for the participants to interact and settle in. The Lapsit program consists of four components:

1. introduction,
2. storytime,
3. adult education,
4. networking and interaction among participants.

The first five minutes or so consists of the general welcome and expectations of the class. It gives the librarian the opportunity to let the adults know it is not expected that the children will sit still. It is a chance to remind adults of guidelines, introduce yourself and participants, and get ready to start storytime. The second part is the actual Lapsit storytime, and the third consists of the parent information, handouts, display and question/answer period. Finally, the fourth component enables networking and dialog between the participants. We will examine each part in closer detail.

## Part 1: Setting the Stage

The introduction is primarily used to create an atmosphere where the adults can relax and enjoy sharing the stories and activities presented with their children. It is sometimes useful to let participants introduce themselves and their children with each child's age. Knowing the age range of the group helps also in knowing their abilities. Group situations tend to lead adults to compare his or her own child with others. It is useful to remind them that each child is unique and develops at his or her own rate. Explaining the general behavior developments and skills of this age group, the librarian reassures the adult that his or her child is really doing just fine. Many parents are overwhelmed when a placid, peaceful infant becomes a whirlwind of activity at the start of exploring mobility. Stating that the children are not expected to sit still tells the adult participants what the librarian expects so they can relax and enjoy the program. It is also possible at this time to set guidelines or "rules". These can be presented in a number of ways:

1. By stating them aloud to the group.
2. Writing them on a poster board, laminating it, posting it on the wall, and then directing the group's attention to it.
3. Printing them on a handout given when participants arrive, and then put aside.

Here are some basic guidelines.

1. Everyone participates, especially the adults. Children take their cue from their caregivers so if they relax and enjoy the program, the children probably will too.
2. Please put toys and food away. They distract your child and others. Bottles or other "not-to-be-parted-with" items are ok, but should be used discreetly. This applies especially to breast feeding.
3. The room has been reserved for us so there will be lots of time to share after the program. Let's get started when the children are fresh.
4. If your child seems overwhelmed, starts to cry or in general "loses it" please feel free to step outside the room for a moment or try again next week. Don't hesitate to discuss with the librarian any concern about your child's behavior.
5. Relax! We don't expect your child to take part in all our activities. The goal is to have fun with rhymes, songs, books and other language-building play.

Ann Carlson Weeks book *Early Childhood Literature Sharing Programs in Libraries*, published in 1985, gives an excellent overview of early childhood development and their implications for library programing. *Please Touch*, by Susan Striker, I found to be very useful in understanding the creative developmental patterns for young children and how to encourage them. *Raising Readers: A Guide to Sharing Literature with Young Children* by Linda Leonard Lamme and others, explains early childhood skills and behavior and how to work with them when introducing literature to children at a young age.

## Part Two: Lapsit Storytime

The second part of the program is the storytime which runs approximately 15 to 25 minutes. It consists of stories from books suitable for the age group, songs, fingergames and rhymes. It is important to be prepared with more material than you will really need , for the key to this program is flexibility. By being prepared, the librarian can create a fun literature-sharing experience using rhymes, fingergames and songs for an active group while the next time the same song may be able to settle in for more stories read aloud. This is where the librarian role models for the adult can encourage reading aloud at home. Parents may know what they are supposed to do and even why but it is often the question "how?" that causes them to falter. A mother seeing her child when he or she is enthralled listening to a story being read aloud, will want that experience for herself—and so will a father, a grandmother or other primary caregiver. They will feel less self-conscious when sharing fingergames, rhymes, stories and songs with the child when they realize there will be no criticism of their talents by the child, only joy in the experience they share. They have also seen another adult, the librarian, interact with their children and have witnessed firsthand how delightful the experience can be. The basic format to the storytime is as follows:

> Opening song.
> Fingergames/rhyme/bounce.
> Story.
> Fingergames/rhyme/bounce, song.
> Story.
> Fingergames/rhyme/bounce, song.
> Story.
> Fingergames/rhyme/bounce.
> Closing song.

By varying the number of fingergames, rhymes, and songs, you can change the length of the program. There should always be one story read aloud to the group and it is possible to read up to three books per program. It may be tempting to increase the time for this part of the program because it really is fun, but keep in mind the children are absorbing everything that is said and done in the class even if they are not actively participating and may become over stimulated. It is best not to cross over that fine line by trying to lengthen and fit too many literary experiences in the time frame. Overstimulated participants cannot savor and absorb as well what has been presented. Leaving the children with a sense of wanting more will more than likely encourage the adults to recreate the literature sharing experience at home. Specific programs and materials can be found in the next section, Adult Education.

## Part Three: Adult Education

The third or parent education and awareness section is really much easier than it sounds. It can be approached in whatever way the librarian desires by booktalking, display or even by simply posing an interesting quote pertaining to reading and children or reason to read to your child and discussing it a little. Displaying books and other materials covering topics the adults have inquired about or would find informative, helps develop their awareness of available materials. These topics could be about general parenting, communicating with children, things to do in or around the area with the child, nursery rhyme books other than Mother Goose, and how to select videos for children. This is also a good time to bring to their attention library services and materials they may not be aware of. More ideas and materials for this section will be in the next chapter. Handouts are distributed at this time because earlier hands will need to be free in order to actively participate with the children during the program. Simple craft items are distributed at this time as well. Tying the craft to some element of verbal sharing between the adult and child encourages them to remember "we got this at the library" during the following week. Keeping the craft simple—for example a fingerpuppet or picture card, encourages the adult to recreate the literature/language sharing experience again and again. Sample crafts and handouts will be supplied in Chapter 7.

**Part Four: Added Bonus**
The fourth and final portion is really the easiest and that is to allow time for interaction and dialog among the participants. This may be the only activity for parents to participate in with their children and have an opportunity to see them interact with others the same age. Books can be browsed through and checked out. Music, age appropriate, can be softly played to create a relaxed atmosphere. If possible board books can be put out for the little ones to examine and "read." It is important for the librarian to be available to answer questions, give a brief tour of the library or perhaps supply resources, and talk individually with adults. Have a pad of paper for questions to be written on. This way, some inquires can be responded to at the next program or by phone during the week. In any case, it helps the parent/adult realize that he or she and the child are welcome and encouraged to use their local library.

## OTHER THINGS TO CONSIDER

In addition to planning the program there are a few other items to take into consideration when venturing into lapsit library service.
   One of the first questions you need to settle about the lapsit program is when would be the best time to schedule it. Most story-

times are offered on a weekday often in the morning because naps are still part of the child's daily routine. If there are few community activities in your area, something like this would be welcome. Depending on when your library opens, it could also be scheduled before opening to allow for the possible increase in noise level during the program. If your situation is that your community consists of many working parents, daytime may not be the best choice. An early evening program, starting by 7:00pm and ending at 7:30pm, is often a better choice. I have found it gives families enough time for supper and getting to the library, by families, yet still isn't too late a bedtime. The storytime section usually ends with a bedtime story, lullaby or quiet song so the children are not over-stimulated. An added bonus to this program time is that parents who normally do not get to the library or spend time sharing group activities with their child can. They begin to think of the library as a fun place to go. Saturdays tend to be reserved for "family time" at home, trips or other pre-planned activities and I have found most working parents are reluctant to attend programs at that time, especially Saturday mornings. Study the habits and needs of your community and select the best time for your program after asking around and doing your homework.

Deciding how often to hold this program must also be taken into consideration. Many participants want to have this program available every week and you may find the demand for more classes increasing. By examining your resources and other commitments, you can set realistic offerings without running yourself ragged or ignoring other areas of service. For example, we offer the evening Lapsit program as a four to five week series twice a year—in the spring and again in the fall. Four other King County libraries, which offer daytime programs, have cooperated so that each library has the program once a month in a different week. This way, their patrons can participate once a month at their home library or weekly by traveling to the other nearby libraries in the system.

Do not forget to consider the size that the group should be for the program to succeed. There is a size limit and that brings up the question of registration, and the pros and cons. Having an "open door" policy can work and can draw high attendance. Remember though that this age group can also be overwhelming in large numbers not only for the librarian but for the children as well. We use registration at the evening Lapsit sessions for a variety of reasons.

1. It helps the adult commit to a specific time and program.
2. With the facility available only so many can fit in the program room.

3. Smaller numbers allows for more interaction between librarian and group.

4. Because the program contains parent education handouts and materials the librarian needs to know how many to create.

5. This program is designed for one adult and one child to interact one-on-one. Older and younger siblings are not encouraged to attend though, two adults with one child works just fine. If younger children are in attendance I encourage the adult to interact with the pretoddler as much as possible and discuss the situation individually with the caregiver after the program. Without sign-up the librarian may have to work with whoever comes—too few or too many.

6. You can use registration to keep in touch with the participants during the week, to answer questions they may have asked, reassure them if they express concerns about how their child's behavior during the program, or touch base if they were absent. With all that parents have to handle in daily coping hearing from the librarian may reinforce the notion that their trip to the library is worth the investment they make.

Consider where the program will be held. In some circumstances the library is the only option. Using a meeting room would be highly recommended due mostly to noise level. Wherever you hold the program try to make it as child-safe as possible. This age group is into exploring so try to remove objects that may topple over, cover electrical outlets and create an environment where everyone can relax. It is often beneficial to indicate the boundaries inside of which the program will actually take place. The use of chairs can enclose an area but they also give the children something to climb on. A quilt or blanket would also serve this purpose but keep in mind your program. Getting up and down off the floor is not as easy as using a chair for many adults. Bouncing rhymes are also easier when done in a chair. Displays are best on a table out of the reach of curious little hands, and displays placed behind the program area are also less distracting. I often bring out a box of board books after the storytime so the children can "read" their own books when the big people can check out the displays.

## TIPS

Before moving onto the programs and materials here are a few tips to keep in mind when organizing your program.

1. Wear clothes in which you have freedom of movement and will not distract people following your actions. Slacks, flat shoes, and a relaxed top seem to be the best suited for this kind

of active program. Jewelry such as shiny necklaces and earrings that dangle are of fascinating for the child this age. Children like to grab for shining or glittering things. Jewelry can also hinder your movements when acting out songs and rhymes such as bouncing like a ball.

2. Pockets are useful to keep fingerpuppets in when not needed so the children will not be distracted by them. A smock or apron serves this purpose also.

3. It is useful to have an opening and closing to create a framework for the program. This can be a song that starts the program and ends it. For, example, clap hands to "the More We Get Together." Children in this age group respond to routine and within a brief period will recognize this indicates storytime is starting. They will begin to direct their attention to the librarian when the clapping and song begin.

4. The librarian is not just a performer or a role model. Information can be interjected about how and when the stories, rhymes, and songs can be utilized and enjoyed by parent and child throughout the program. The enthusiasm for literature and language that the librarian displays has been found to be very contagious. Many families catch the "reading is fun" bug and then become regular library users.

# PROGRAMS AND MATERIALS

When putting together your program it will be useful to keep the following points in mind. If possible, create a flow to your program that seems natural and does not demand excessive activities which may cause distraction—for example, after a story the children may be getting restless and need to stand and stretch. Stand for "the Great Big Spider," and then do "Tall as a Pin" that will bring you back down to the floor where you can do "Jack in the Box" and end with "Cobbler, Cobbler Mend My Shoe." At this point you are sitting down, quiet and ready for another song or story. Try to begin your program simply, have a variety of material to present and aim for a calming or quieter conclusion if possible. Ending the program with the children overstimulated and parents tense is not a good idea.

Repeating fingergames and rhymes is perfectly ok because many children have favorites and love to do them repeatedly. Plan to repeat rhymes and fingergames at least two to three times. Repetition is a wonderful learning device and also serves to refresh the adults' memories of their own childhood rhymes.

Use an index card with the names of rhymes, stories, and songs, you plan to use. This is helpful to keep the flow of the program moving along. This way you do not have to rely only on memory. Keep this card in your pocket or near your materials for easy reference.

Concerning the materials used, some adults may find the version they learned or remember is not same as what is presented. Respond to their concern by telling them about the existence of what can be called a "family vocabulary." Each family may have a word or phrase that is uniquely its own. For example, in our family we had "white salt" and certain melodies to rhymes. It is acceptable for others to create special rhymes, songs, and stories that work for their families as well.

Sound has become a fascination for many children this age and they love to use it especially when it rhymes. If an adult expresses concern about saying a rhyme correctly or his/her child is mixing the words up, give reassurance that it is absolutely ok. The adult is helping the child build a love for words and increases their confidence in using the language skills. Children are learning when they begin to verbalize and create rhymes on their own.

Keep in mind where you will arrange your books and materials during the program. Children in this age range love to touch and explore everything. If you are using a doll or a large stuffed animal think of where it can be put so the children will not be distracted by it. Fingerpuppets that disappear into a pocket or bag work great. Larger puppets you may use to enhance your rhymes or songs need to also be placed out of temptation's reach when you are finished with them. Keeping your materials on a table, in a box out of the children's reach or out of sight will help keep the children's attention centered on the librarian.

The children may want to hold or touch the book you are reading rather than listen to the story. Gently, but firmly, you can redirect the child's attention back to the story by using your voice, facial expressions, direct eye contact and verbal direction, such as "(Child's name) Please sit so everyone can see." There are also other ways to help bring the child's attention back to the activity presently being done in the class. Using surprise will catch the child's attention and direct it back to what you are sharing. For example, barking like a dog when the white dog appears in *Brown Bear, Brown Bear What Do You See?* by Bill Martin Jr., never fails to draw the child's attention back to the story to see the dog and anticipate what is on the next page. Singing a familiar song will also help the children focus on what you are doing especially if you have discovered a favorite. Go right ahead and use the song more than one time during the program if need to be. Children respond favorably to rhyme whether it appears in a story, song, or poem. Finally, touch that is non-threatening and gentle can draw a child's attention back to the group. For example a touch on the shoulder may encourage someone to sit down or ask another to hug his special adult will bring them back to focus upon what is happening in the group. Most of all, remember to be flexible and have fun!

## BOOKS

What kind of story works best with this age group and how many stories should you plan to use during a Lapsit? Be selective when choosing the books you use. As you use them you will discover your own favorites. Do not worry about using them over and over again, even within the same series. One obvious reason is that if you enjoy the story you will be able to read it expressively and not be tied to the print on the page. Another reason is that it becomes familiar to the children and they can respond to the story. Children need time to absorb what is being said and shown. This is difficult to do with only one brief encounter. Thirdly, any adult with a child this age will tell you that familiar and favorite stories can never be read often enough to suit the child. Repetition is how children grow in becoming familiar with a story, learning the story, sharing the story, and eventually wanting to learn how to read the story. If you are conducting a series of Lapsits, select one title that you use each week. It helps set a routine the children become familiar and comfortable with. Children can also develop a sense of anticipation by knowing what the story is about.

Keep in mind the size of the book, how involved the text is and its illustrations. Select books that can be easily seen by a group. If the book is too small the illustrations will not catch and hold the children's attention. With the availability of oversized "big" books, this may not seem like a problem but the librarian must be able to manipulate them. There are many wonderful stories to share with this age group but not all work best in a group setting. Some books are best one on one. They can be recommended as such and incorporated into a display.

The story line should be clear and simple. Illustrations that are bright, clear and colorful seem to work best. Poetry and songs that have been made into picturebooks are good books to use as well.

The length of the text is important to keep in mind. If the Lapsit is short, the children are overly zealous or a definite favorite is in demand it is just fine to repeat a story within the same program. The text can be in rhyme, animal sounds, or simple sentences. Use your voice to help the text come to life and stir the child and adult who hears it. We plan on three different stories per Lapsit but usually have a few more titles that enable flexibility within the program. Here are some favorite books to use:

1. *Brown Bear, Brown Bear* by Bill Martin, Jr. Published in 1983 it is a favorite and familiar title with many families. If this is a story that has been read at home the child is able to tie the library environment to the home environment as a place to share fun experience with parents. If it is a new title it becomes popular through the librarian's presentation. Because it is easy to incorporate animal sounds in the story this title is a good one for the librarian to use as a role model for reading with expression. Because the story is in rhyme and relatively easy to learn, the librarian is able to have greater eye contact and communication with the group to help them relax and enjoy the story.

2. *Where's Spot?* by Eric Hill. Eric Hill's flap board books can be wonderful to use because they are brief, sturdy and have good illustrations. The ones involving simple story plots work the best — for example, looking for Spot or going to the farm. Make sure the book and flaps have been opened prior to reading because they can be stiff when first used.

3. *I Hear* by Rachel Isadora is a great concept book to use. I like to use this one because the children respond to the sounds used when I am reading the text. Isadora is an author many adults do not know and the length of the story is perfect for the very young child. Her books are also available in board book form which enhances their durability.

4. *The Box With Red Wheels* by Maud and Miska Petersham is another good title. Although out of print, it is available in paperback form. The red borders, clear pictures, and gentle text blanket the listeners in a warm inviting story. It is a book often overlooked by many adults and by using it the librarian introduces it to those who may never have heard it.

5. *The Little Mouse, The Red, Ripe Strawberry, And The Big, Hungry Bear* by Don and Audrey Woods. I include this title not only for the children but the adults as well. It clearly illustrates that picturebooks can be fun for everyone no matter what their age. The little ones love to look for the strawberry and the adults love the surprise disguise. Needless to say the librarian can be very dramatic in the reading. It is just plain fun!

6. *Grandfather Twilight* by Barbara Berger is one I use as an alternative to *Goodnight Moon* by Margaret Wise Brown. Brown's book is a classic and most people are familiar with it. Berger's book is unusual and a good one to make people aware of. Its quiet twilight walk settles the children down and the illustrations give them things to look for, such as the bunnies by the stream. Use it as the closing story for the evening Lapsit and bring the program to a relaxed, quiet conclusion before your closing song.

## Recommended Titles to Use for Lapsit:

Bang, Molly. *Ten, Nine, Eight.* New York: Greenwillow Books, 1983.

Berger, Barbara. *Grandfather Twilight.* New York: Philomel Books, 1984.

Brown, Margaret Wise. *Goodnight Moon.* Illus. by Clement Hurd. New York: Harper and Row, Publishers, 1947, 1975.

Butterworth, Nick and Mick Inkpen. *Just Like Jasper.* Boston: Little, Brown and Company, 1989.

Campbell, Rod. *Dear Zoo.* New York: Four Winds Press, 1983, c1982.

Flack. *Angus and the Ducks.* New York: Doubleday, Doran and Company, Inc., 1930.

Florian, Douglas. *At the Zoo.* New York: Greenwillow, 1992.

Ginsburg, Mirra. *Good Morning Chick.* New York: Greenwillow, 1980.

Hale, Sarah Josepha. *Mary Had A Little Lamb.* illustrated. by Bruce McMillan. New York: Scholastic Inc., 1990.

Hill, Eric. *Spot On The Farm.* New York: G.P. Putnam's Sons, 19

Hill, Eric. *Where's Spot?* New York: G.P. Putnam's Sons, 1980.

Hoban, Tana. *One, Two, Three.* New York: Greenwillow, 1985.

Hoban, Tana, *What Is It?* New York: Greenwillow, 1985.

Holzenthaler, Jean. *My Hands Can.* Illustrated. by Nancy Tafuri. New York: E.P. Dutton, 1978.

Hutchins, Pat. *Goodnight Owl.* New York: Macmillan, 1972.

Isadora, Rachel. *I Hear.* New York: Greenwillow, 1985.

Krauss, Ruth. *Happy Day.* New York: HarperCollins Children's Books, 1949.

Krauss, Ruth. *The Carrot Seed.* Illustrated by Crockett Johnson. Harper and Row, Publishers, Inc., 1945.

Kunhardt, Dorothy. *Pat the Bunny.* New York: Golden, 1940.

Martin, Bill, Jr. *Brown Bear, Brown Bear, What Do You See?* Illustrated. by Eric Carle. New York: Henry Holt and Company, 1967, 1983.

Martin, Bill, Jr. and John Archambault. *Here Are My Hands.* Illustrated by Ted Rand. New York: Henry Holt and Company, 1987.

Ormerod, Jan. *The Saucepan Game.* New York: Lothrop, Lee and Shepard, 1989.

Oxenbury, Helen. *All Fall Down.* New York: Aladdin, 1987.

Oxenbury, Helen. *Clap Hands.* New York: Aladdin, 1987.

Polushkin, Maria. *Who Said Meow?* New York: Bradbury Press, 1988.

Rojankovsky, Feodor. *Animals On The Farm.* New York: Knopf, 1967.

Rice, Eve. *Benny Bakes A Cake.* New York: Greenwillow, 1981.

Rice, Eve. *Sam Who Never Forgets.* New York: Greenwillow Books, 1977.

Risom, Ole. *I Am A Bunny.* Illustrated by Richard Scarry. New York: Golden Book, 1963.

Scott, Ann Herbert. *On Mother's Lap.* New York: Greenwillow Books, 1972.

Shaw, Charles. *It Looked Like Spilt Milk.* New York: Harper Collins Children's Books, 1992.

Tafuri, Nancy. *Have You Seen My Duckling?* New York: Greenwillow, 1984.

Watanabe, Shigeo. *How Do I Put It On?* New York: Putnum Publishing Group, 1984.

Wood, Don and Audrey Wood. *The Little Mouse, the Red Ripe Strawberry and the Big Hungry Bear.* Child's Play (International) Ltd., 1984.

Wood, Don and Audrey Wood. *Piggies.* San Diego: Harcout Brace Jovanovich, 1991.

## FINGERGAMES RHYMES

The importance of fingergames or fingerrhymes is often underestimated by many adults. They may be looked upon as silly things to do and may even cause the adult embarrassment when doing these simple rhymes. They do, however, have an important purpose in the development of language for the child. By using nursery rhymes and fingergames the adult actively engages the child in the language learning experience. "Children need to have experiences before they can attach words to the experiences" and "Children must be actively involved to learn" are two statements made by Bev Bos in *Before the Basics*. These statements indicate how important it is that the adult share in the learning experience with the child and help involve him or her in it to the fulliest extent possible. Together the adult and child share the world of language in rhyme, song and story. Fingergames also aid the child in learning the important skills involved in listening. The child will grow in his or her ability to listen, comprehend directions, follow the directions, and act on them. Children need to have listening skills prior to comprehension and reading skills. With each repetition the rhyme becomes more familiar to the participants and thus they gain confidence in speaking the rhyme themselves.

When using fingergames and rhymes in the Lapsit program it is best to use a core collection of familiar rhymes and add a few new ones each time. The children, as well as the adults, will recognize the familiar ones, and because they can do those they will be less hesitant to try the unfamiliar newer rhymes.

There are various ways to introduce a rhyme or fingergame. Find which method suits you best and then use it. It is best to treat the rhyme as new to everyone attending the program. This is especially true when the group consists of various cultures, including those for which, English is the second language. Whichever method you use, speak clearly and explain the directions for the movements involved in simple terms. One method is to state each line of the rhyme or fingergame one at a time and describe the action for it. Have the participants do that line with you leading the group. After the entire rhyme/fingergame is presented, the entire group can go through the whole rhyme/fingergame together. A second method is for the leader to say the desired rhyme/fingergame in its entirety as he or she is demonstrating the actions that go with it at the same time. The group can then repeat the rhyme/fingergame together. A third method is to use audio materials that are available. For example, *The Baby Record* by Bob McGrath and Katharine Smithrim is excellent for aiding you to become familiar with method one. The selection of rhymes and fingergames, quality of the sound track and clear presentation by these two artists make this an useful support to learning the rhyme/fingergame. However you may find that when the group has learned the desired rhyme/fingergame, this may seem too directive for group use. Nancy Stewart has produced Little Songs For Little Me, and uses vocals and a simple guitar background to present the entire rhyme/fingergame. This can be utilized for method two if you feel your voice needs backup. The tape can be played as the leader demonstrates the actions involved.

Learning the words can be done by various methods as well. One method is printing the words on posters and tacking them up on the walls in the front of the room. Encourage the adults to not rely on these printed signs any longer than necessary because you want them to center their attention on interacting with their children, not a poster on the wall. Another method is printing the words for the rhyme/fingergames and directions on a sheet of paper and using them as a handout. It is not necessary to include every rhyme/fingergame used, usually one or two will satisfy the participants especially if they are the least familiar ones you used during the program.

Rhymes and fingergames are often adapted to the speed or rhyme of whoever is doing them. By acknowledging the fact that there are various ways to say and act out a rhyme you, in a sense, give the participants permission to be comfortable with the way "they do" the rhyme or fingergame. This not only reinforces the participant's own experiences, but also engages their assistance in creating a program that involves them. It gives the adults a chance to share their own knowledge and experience within the group. You can also demonstrate the various ways a rhyme/fingergame can be acted out. "This Little Piggy" is known by most American families and the usual toes or fingers are tickled and wiggled in the appropriate places. It can also be done by using the child's entire limb, leg, arm and even belly to produce the same enjoyment. This presentation works with younger children who are ready to work on developing their large motor skills. Encourage adults to help their children experience the rhyme/fingergame by aiding their childs movements and thus experiencing it with their senses.

The age span of children for the Lapsit program may result in having pre-crawlers with non-stop movers in the same group. Many parents may feel their child is not actively participating even if they are moving about. It is best to remember and reassure the adults that the children are receiving or being made aware of words, rhythm, and rhyme by just being there. Introducing the world of language and literature to children at an early age gives them a greater chance to develop their skills of listening, and comprehension. Children must first be exposed to the world of language in order to learn about it. They learn by observing and absorbing the experiences around them. Slowly, they will begin to participate at their own pace and when they are ready. The Lapsit program is an excellent way to expose children to the language experience.

## RECOMMENDED TITLES

The following are rhymes and fingergames to use for a Lapsit program and resources in which to find more.

Beall, Parelan. *Wee Sing: Children's Songs and Fingerplays*. Los Angeles: Price/Stern/Sloan, 1979.

Defty, Jeff. *Creative Fingerplays and Action Rhymes: An Index and Guide to Their Use.* Phoenix, Arizionia: Oryx Press, 1992.

Flint Michigan Public Library. *Ring A Ring O'Roses.* Flint Public Library.

Glazer, Tom. *Eye Winker, Tom Tinker, Chin Chopper: Fifty Musical Fingerplays.* Garden City N.Y.: Doubleday, 1973, 1978.

Glazer, Tom. *Music for Ones and Twos: Songs and Games for the Very Young Child.* Garden City, N.Y.: Doubleday, 1983.

Grayson, Marion. *Let's Do Fingerplays.* R.B. Luce, 1962.

McGrath, Bob and Katharine Smithrim. *The Baby Record.* Toronto, Ontario: Kids' Records, 1983.

McGrath, Bob and Katharine Smithrim. *Songs and Games For Toddlers.* Toronto, Ontario: Kids' Records, 1985.

Montgomerie, Norah, Comp. *This Little Pig Went To Market: Play Rhymes For Infants and Young Children.* Illus. by Margery Gill. London: Bodley Head, 1983, 1966.

Ra, Carol F., comp. *Trot, Trot To Boston: Play Rhymes For Baby.* New York: Lothrop, Lee and Shepard Books, 1987.

Stewart, Nancy. *Little Songs For Little Me: Activity Songs For Ones and Twos.* Mercer Island, Friends Street Music, 1992.

Watson, Clyde. *Catch Me and Kiss Me and Say It again.* New York: Collins + World, 1978.

## MUSIC

The very first source of music a child experiences is the internal vibrations and sounds when in the mother's womb. The rhythm and sounds encompass their very existence. "Music is a language that uses tones and rhythm to express communication." (*Your Children Need Music* by Marvin Greenberg). Once separated from these methods of communication the child naturally is drawn towards music whenever exposed to it. As the child grows so does his or her ability to respond and emulate, first, by listening to sounds, and then experimenting with the sounds (ie. babbling or cooing) and finally actively participating with verbalization and moving to the rhythm. With time and exposure the child increases in ability to express self using rhythm and sounds.

Music can serve many functions in addition to being used for simple enjoyment. It can be used in a calming and soothing manner to settle a cranky or overstimnulated child, introduce concepts such as fast-slow, loud-soft; supply background for a familiar activity; and gain the child's cooperation even encouraging development of musical capabilities. Here are some examples:

1. Lullabies or quiet classical music to calm or settle a child.
2. Marches or drums to release energy or to encourage the child to continue walking instead of being carried.
3. Change pitch or rhythm of voice as you are reading stories or saying rhymes to demonstrate concepts such as high-low, fast-slow, etc.
4. Introduce parts of the day by using a song. For example, "Rub-a-dub-dub, three men in a tub" for bathtime or "Shoe the old horse" while changing a diaper.
5. When singing a song or fingergame, vary the speed in which you do it and tell the child what you intend to do. For example, sing "Row, Row, Row Your Boat" at a normal speed, then repeat it fast, and then slow. Remember to tell the child each time what speed you are going use. Be prepared to discover your child's preferred pace.

The child passes through different stages of musical awareness and develops various responses while growing in abilities. The infant responds to sounds by visually turning to the stimulus, learns to discriminate between different sounds such as mother's higher pitched and daddy's lower pitched voice, and by imitating sounds by using his or her own voice. The adult can actively involve the child in the music experience by physically clapping the child's hands together and creating a simple pattern of beats. By age one the child has gained a greater control over motor skills and explores a larger area. Holding simple rhythm instruments is now possible, but the child is still learning what is permitted in using an instrument—for example, using a wooden spoon to hit a pot is ok, but not to hit Mommy! By age two the child is growing in ability to control their own voice, imitate rhythm patterns, and follow actions described in songs. Keep in mind, all children develop in their own unique way but they do follow a general pattern. They first begin by verbalizing sounds, and then experiment by using the voice and being able to imitate sounds. An approximation of singing begins after the first year and usually by the age of three to four singing accurately within a limited range has been achieved.

Incorporating action and the child's involvement into the musical experience also takes time to develop. Initially, fingergames are used where the adult helps the child act out the story, song or rhyme. This is illustrated by the rhymes: "this little piggy" or "Pat a cake" as perhaps the first fingergames between parent and child.

This interaction progresses to action songs that require appropriate movements rather than learned patterns—for example, "This Old Man."

The adult has an important role to play during this early musical development for the child. Music needs to be experienced in the daily life of the child at home. Music in the home can take various forms, as follows:

1. Through frequent singing/humming/cooing aloud by the caregiver.
2. Rhythmically moving to music as the child is being held by the caregiver.
3. Letting the child play with home style instruments such as a wooden spoon and pot.
4. Reading nursery rhymes and chants.
5. Enabling the child to hear music through the use of tape recordings of selected television or radio shows, or outings where sounds can be experienced such as the zoo, a concert, etc.

According to Marvin Greenberg in his book Your Children Need Music there are three basic experiences in music that are needed for aesthetic growth:

1. listen to music,
2. perform music and
3. create music.

The adult can expose the child to various listening to various types of music ranging from Old MacDonald to classical. Performing music can be accomplished by chanting names, banging blocks to songs such as "Row, Row, Row Your Boat" or singing songs together like "If You're Happy and You Know It Clap Your Hands." Creating music is occurring throughout this period when the infant first plays with inflections and the sounds, of his own voice—the one year old changing the beating pattern on his or her and the older child singing a male-up song aloud. The adult encourages by providing an environment that will nurture the creativity of the child, such as sounds, to initiate playing an instrument. Recognizing the unique individuality of each child, the adult must learn to allow time for experiences to be absorbed and to be able to take advantage of any occasion by incorporating music into it. It is important to remember the child's point of view and not try to impose adult standards on it. Enjoy the process of creating rather than concentrating on the results.

The librarian fits into this area as a resource and guide. Many adults are overly self conscious of their singing abilities and refuse to attempt to sing a note. Supplying simple tunes and songs, wonderful tapes and other quality media, and being a role model the librarian can help the adult introduce music to his or her child. The adult may not like the sound of her own voice but children are not critical and will listen to many different sounds. Crooning, involving only a few sounds and pitches can be learned or at least attempted by almost anyone. Encouraging adults to accept their own abilities, just as a child will, may be an important goal of the librarian. Librarians can supply lists of nursery tunes, classical music, ethnic music, jazz, folk, sounds of the world and other varieties of music which adults can try out at home prior to purchasing materials to keep. Assorted recorded bird songs are good for imitation.

Using media during the Lapsit program, as well as before and after, can be done in various ways, as follows:

1. Make sure the equipment is set up in a safe area where the children cannot upset it or be exposed to wiring.
2. Make sure it is ready to play so there will be as little break in the routine as possible.
3. Check the volume before turning it on.
4. Actively involve the group in music rather than just listening to it. This can be done by the child being held and rocked to music, moving to the music by the group as a whole, march, swing or sway and even by simply clapping along with the beat.
5. Keep the music period brief so that the mood or response is no longer than two minutes or so.
6. Picturebooks have been created based on songs and these can be used during the program as well. A partial list of these titles follows this section.

Titles available in the area of children's materials have grown in number during the past few years and there are a large variety of formats. Cassettes are usually of good quality and reasonably priced. Records are loosing popularity although daycares, schools, and some homes still prefer them because CD's are somewhat more expensive. However the number of children's titles are growing and more performers are utilizing this technology.

Librarians and libraries enable adults to sample and select what they wish their children to experience in the realm of music, rhyme and sound.

## PUPPETS

The use of puppets can greatly enhance your program. They should not create a distraction for the children when not in use however. A doll or a large stuffed animal with movable joints can be used to demonstrate fingergames and action rhymes. By using this puppet or doll the librarian can demonstrate the actions appropriate for this age group as well as various adaptations of the actions for different age groups. If possible, keep out of the children's reach when you are doing other things so the group can concentrate on what you are currently sharing. Since this object is usually in the presenter's possession it is often possible to hide it under a blanket until it is time for it to be a stage. Children at this age may have strong feeling towards this puppet so be sensitive to the group. Some children may want to hug and love it, others fearful of it. Take these possibilties consideration when selecting a "partner" puppet.

Fingerpuppets, I have found, have advantages over the larger puppets. Due to their size they can disappear quickly into a pocket, are large enough for the group to see, yet small enough to make them focus on the presenter, and they can be created or purchased reasonably. For example, lets examine the familiar fingergame of "Two Little Blackbirds." The rhyme states:

> "Two little blackbirds sitting on a hill.
> One named Jack, the other named Jill.
> Fly away Jack, fly away Jill.
> Come back Jack, come back Jill."

We use two fingerpuppets that were purchased at a local craft bazaar, which is where many such items can be found. You could also cut two pictures of blackbirds out of a magazine, glue rings of paper on them and use these as fingerpuppets. Hands can also be used by touching thumb to fingertips and making beak shapes which could be enhanced by black dots put in the eye area. Fingerpuppets can also be created as a handout distributed after the program to be taken home to recreate the experience there. Here are some resources for fingerpuppets:

*Easy to Make Puppets and How to Use Them . . . Early Childhood.* Fran Rottman. Ventura, California: Regal Books, a division of GL Publications, 1978.

*Fingerpuppets, Fingerplays and Holidays.* Betty Keefe. Omaha, Neb.: Special Literature Press, 1984.

*Mit Magic: fingerplays for finger puppets.* Lynda Roberts. Mt. Rainier, MD: Gryphon House, 1985.

*Pocketful of Puppets: Mother Goose.* Iamara Hunt and Nancy Renfro. Austin, Texas.: Nancy Renfro Studios, 1992.

*Puppetry In Early Childhood Education.* Iamara Hunt and Nancy Renfro. Austin, Texas.: Nancy Renfro Studios, 1982.

*Puppets With Pazazz: 52 finger and hand puppets children can make and use.* Joy Wilt, Owen Hurn and John Hurn. Waco, Texas.: Creative Resources, 1977.

## OTHER MATERIALS—(Felt boards, pass around books etc.)

Librarians are always on the lookout for various ways to present stories and rhymes. Two ways that are possible are felt board presentations and what I call "pass around books".

Felt boards and the use of felt pieces enable the story or rhyme to be seen by a larger group. Felt pieces are safe for the children to interact with as well. Using this method of presentation it is relatively easy to illustrate such songs as "Old MacDonald Had A Farm" and stories like *The Carrot Seed* by Krauss. Other demonstrations could include concepts such as big and little , colors, and patterns. It is even possible that smaller felt boards could be created for the class to use during the program so members could recreate what the librarian shares.

A "pass around book" is not necessarily an oversized book that the group shares but one that is shared page by page. *Pat The Bunny* by Dorothy Kunhardt is a title that many parents are already familiar with. It is not usually used in a group situation due to the necessity of touching each page and its small size. By recreating each page on a larger scale and adding the texture in the proper places the librarian can pass each page around the group so all can experience the book.

Another method to use when presenting a story is to use props. It is in a sense acting out the story instead of just reading or telling it. *Now We Can Go* by Ann Jonas is one that works well using this method. The various items can be put in a box, and then transferred to a tote bag or other carrier as the story progresses.

Using stuffed animals when you are singing "Old MacDonald" had a farm is another way to increase the interest and involvment of the children in the program.

Publishers are also printing what they call Big Books or oversize books which are useful to use with large groups. They do demand dexterity to use because they are very large. An easel can be used to help hold the book, but remember to make sure it is in a safe place and cannot be tipped over by the children. Some publishers that produce such books are Scholastic Books, Harper-Collins, Morrow, Penguin, Aladdin, Harcourt Brace, and Henry Holt.

The important thing to remember when incorporating these into your program is to make sure they don't become a distraction. Do the children grab for the pieces, refuse to give them up or refuse to move on to the next item on your agenda? Make sure you are aware of the personality of your group. If you feel comfortable with the reactions to these interactive materials, then make them a part of your program.

# WAYS TO ENHANCE YOUR PROGRAM

Handouts, displays, and simple crafts are ways to make your program unique and enable the adults to recreate the literature sharing time they experience during Lapsit in their own home. It does necessitate additional preparation time but the advantages of investing in the effort are numerous. When created the handouts can be duplicated for future programs and even incorporated into other programs such as speaking to daycare providers and used at a "literacy fair" to promote reading to the very young child. Handouts supporting the importance or reading to children at a very young age may exist but have always reached their intended audience. Books and materials such as audio tapes, videos, free newspapers, etc. can be brought to the patrons who would benefit from them the most and in all likelihood never even knew this material existed.

The craft aspects may be considered by some people to be superfluous but we believe that this is not so. The simple craft is often what makes an impression on the adult. It clearly illustrates how important the library believes it is for language in all formats to be shared by children at a very young age and their caring adults. Investing time in an easy project, using safe and ordinary materials and instructing on how to best utilize the craft gives the participants a "goodie" and helps create a positive attitude towards the library. The additional effort of handouts, displays, and crafts pays off with patrons who become familiar with the library, and its services and feel that this is a place where they want to be. It also encourages the adult to recreate the Lapsit experience at home on their own with the child. If all of this sounds like more than you want to get involved in hold on! It is not as difficult or time consuming as it first appears. Remember, once these have been created you can use them again and again with different groups.

Let's look at each "enhancer" to find out what is really involved in providing it.

## HANDOUTS

Handouts can be a blessing and a curse for many people. They are in high demand for the Lapsit programs, yet can often overwhelm those people who receive them and the people who prepare them. One must balance the time it takes to develop handouts with their value to the real function they are intended to serve. In the case of Lapsit materials, handouts are more than likely to serve as an introduction rather than an end. They are used to directing the patron to resources and helping them to develop literacy awareness within their family's home environment. Many adults take handouts, and then never use them. Librarians should remember to keep handouts simple and easy to understand in order to have them utilized in the most effective manner.

For our four to five week series of Lapsit programs we have developed a variety of handouts that, after initially created, have been relatively easy to update and repeat when necessary. They can be used for monthly programs as well. No matter what kind of program yours is—monthly or weekly—the following handouts should be available for the customers.

1. The library's open hours. The hours are important for letting the parents or caregiver know when the library is available to them. Special phone numbers your library may have are usually included on this form as well, for example, a phone number which can be used to renew materials by phone or connect the patron with a special collection such as a film library.

2. Library card applications. Applications should be available for the patron in the Lapsit immediate area. Some people feel it is too difficult to get into the library with their little ones and this way you are meeting their desire for a library card right then and there.

3. Your business card if you have one. Business cards or something with a contact person's name and phone number on it are very useful items to distribute. Some people may be intimidated by libraries and feel more welcome knowing the children's librarian's name the next time they come in or call.

4. Any newsletter or publication your library may have. This helps the patron become aware of what the library is doing beyond their initial interest.

These four handouts let patrons know when the library is available, perhaps some special services they could take advantage of, a contact person's name and what else the library is doing for others in their community. If they are unable to continue with the Lapsit program, they at least will have this information which may help them to utilize the library and its resources in some other way.

Other handouts can include a welcome sheet that gives a general overview of the class and guidelines to set the adult's minds at rest about what can be expected. The one we use states in bold print right on top: "Welcome Everybody! How do you do?!" and on the bottom: "This is a special library time just for you!" Between these two statements we list some guidelines of what is expected to take place during Lapsit. These guidelines or rules are stated in the program outline section. You need not use handouts for this and if preferred a poster would suffice. It does help create a more relaxed atmosphere however when adults understand the kind of behavior the librarian expects from the children and the adults.

Fingergames and simple rhymes can be typed on a sheet for the adults to take home. Children this age don't mind if some of the words are not the authentic ones. It is the adults who feel they must say it correctly. An important aspect of the Lapsit program is that it gives the adult a chance to see that it is ok to make up your own rhyme. It is also hard to remember everything that was said during a Lapsit or the exact words to a specific rhyme at home during the week, so having a copy of rhymes used as well as perhaps an audio tape of them is also useful. It shows the library really means to help.

Art and craft recipes covering such things as fingerpaint, edible playdough, glue and paint are sought after by adults who have pre-toddler children or work with them. Handouts of this kind can be compiled from various crafts books and a few suggested titles are always a good addition to this handout. Directions for craft projects, especially if they are easy and quick to do, are sought after by adults who have limited time to "be creative" and may not have the funds to buy the more expensive educational or elaborate toys on the market. If even these types of handouts seem to demand too much preparation by the librarian, check around to see if there are book jackets available. By putting out the jackets with suggestions for their use (such as posters, picture cards, etc. See craft section in chapter) the librarian has a useful handout that ties in books and crafts painlessly. This tie-in can be accomplished by suggesting various ways to use the posters or bookjackets in addition to the obvious decorative ones. Recommend checking out the book that is portrayed, talk about what the cover depicts, and encourage a shared experience, for example going to the zoo. These simple reminders help to bring stories and books into the daily life of busy families.

A handout that I have found much in demand by the adult participants is the review sheet of the materials used in the Lapsit class. It includes suggested authors/titles for sharing with their children, what to keep in mind when selecting books for children this age and some general resources they might find useful to reinforce the language sharing with the child.

There is one handout about which there is some question and that is the evaluation sheet. It is usually given out before the last class and its importance is stressed. When first starting Lapsit programming the evaluation sheet was useful to find out where improvements were needed and what areas should be worked on or adjusted. Evaluations also came into use when deciding priorities for programming at our local library. It was valuable to have in writing the support of adults who wanted this kind of library service to continue. Surprisingly, over the years about 75 percent to 85 percent of the evaluations are returned and all of them very supportive. To encourage their return we also include a self-addressed envelope with the evaluation. Questions that are asked in the evaluation include:

1. How old is your child?
2. How many Lapsit classes did you attend—all/half/one.
3. What did you like best about the program?
4. What did you like least about the program?
5. Did it meet your expectations?
6. Have you used any of the ideas presented at home?
7. Did you think the materials were suitable for the age range?
8. Was the time relatively convenient?
9. If offered again, would you attend this class?
10. Suggestions and/or comments.

Handouts don't need to be elaborate. They can be booklists already available in your library or created for this age group. Pathfinders, that help the adult locate materials in the library, can be included for in this area as well. Your library may also receive multiple copies of newspapers or magazines aimed at parents or adults working with this age group. Park district activities, community college booklets, farm guides are all items that fit the definition of handouts that help the adult become aware of the library and community services around them that they can share with their children. An easy handout could be the words of a fingergame or songs with the outline of a fingerpuppet to use with it.

For example, if "The Speckled Frog" song is used during the Lapsit just use a half sheet of paper to put the words on, then outline a frog fingerpuppet next to it that can be colored and cut out at home. (See craft section) If funds are available, handouts can also be purchased from the American Library Association, the National Association For The Education of Young Children or other groups that offer materials encouraging adults to read to the very young child.

Handouts may be items already available in the library or special booklets created just for the program. They can be as detailed as the librarian wants them to be or has the time to make them. Through them all, the thread of a caring adult sharing stories, songs and rhymes with the very young child can all be interwoven by the librarian who believes that one is never too young to learn to love the world of language and books.

## DISPLAYS

Displays, as in the case of handouts, can be as simple or elaborate as the librarian wishes them to be. Factors that determine the displays are:

1. Is there room for a display? Displays are best up on a table up out of the reach of curious little hands. Tables are the good solution unless they limit the activity area too much. This program needs space to move so keep the table in the back if possible so it is not distracting to the participants. Tablecloths are not recommended because they can be pulled off along with everything on them. Displays can be out in the library area which allows for more room to do the program in and also can encourages the participants to explore the library afterwards. If the program takes place in the library itself use a box or basket in which to keep the materials until that section of the program.

2. How much time does the librarian have to gather the display materials? It doesn't need to take an exhorbitant amount of time. Select various books from areas of the library parents might find informative. General parenting books are a good place to start and from there the topics can come from the participants themselves as well as the librarian's knowledge of the collection. Adoption, communicating with children, how to discipline, working parents, books that support the adult (such as being nice to yourself), rhyming books besides Mother Goose, things to do with children in the area are only the tip of the iceberg as to possible display topics. Remember the display is to be a sample not everything the library owns. If specific titles are needed, additional planning is necessary but often a walk through the stacks is sufficient.

3. What kind of material to display? When selecting materials remember to include non-print materials such as tapes, videos, etc. along with resources on how to use them and select them. Adults are not always up to date on the newest and latest in the children's

area of media. It is a chance for the librarian to promote quality media and give suggestions on how to incorporate it properly in the lives of children and adults.

Materials may also be selected to demonstrate the development and changes within a genre that adults may not be aware of leaving their own childhood. Three topics I have used are "Besides Mother Goose", "ABC Books", and *"Variations of a Story"*. Sounds impressive and time consuming but in reality very simple. *"Besides Mother Goose,"* consists of different rhyme books such as Watson's *Catch Me and Kiss Me and Say It Again!,* Jack Prelutsky's *Read-Aloud Rhymes For the Very Young* and individual poems that have been made into picturebooks. I have used Wanda Gag's *ABC Bunny,* Tana Hoban's *26 Letters and 99 cents* and Bill Martin Jr.'s *Chicka Chicka Boom Boom,* to illustrate various types of abc books available.

*"Variations of a Story"* can be shown by using the story poem "The Owl and The Pussycat" by Edward Lear. This poem is available in many forms, as a board book, as part of poetry collections and there are two excellent picturebooks of it still available, one illustrated and retold by Paul Galdone and the other by Jan Brett.

Magazines are also an easy way to create a display. Many adults are not aware of how many parenting magazines are available or that some magazines have sections they would find useful. Even a display of children's magazines would be of interest for examination since subscriptions may be beyond the reach of some new parents and even experienced ones. By letting people know about the periodical collection the librarian is enabling them to view current material whether they can subscribe to a specific magazine or not.

Displays may also cover such topics as award winning picturebooks, "the best" titles for children ages 12 to 24 months, great board books and even titles that remind the adults of books they enjoyed as children. These types of displays are relatively easy to put together and present a great way to show patrons what the library has.

The final display possibility to bring to your attention is in a sense a personal one. Many adults have asked what books would I include as part of a "good child's home library". The librarian can select materials from the collection as possible "core" materials. I bring books from my daughters collection. For some reason, the adults feel reassured that after seeing clothbooks, paperbacks, books worn with use and those of lesser quality than literary best in a children's librarian's home collection, it is fine for their own home library too.

Displays are not an absolute necessity for this program however, let me close with these evaluation comments: In reply to the question about if the materials were suitable for the age range one mother said, "Yes! (the librarian) discovered and brought to our attention wonderful books and tapes, etc. that we would have spent months finding on our own!" And a father stated, "I appreciated the book displays in back of the room. Pre-selection makes it easier to fine age appropriate materials for checking out. Thanks." Many adults agree they never realized the extent of what the library could offer until they had seen a sample of its resources.

## CRAFTS

With all you have done already, why in the world add this to the list of things to do! There are a number of reasons for including a very, very simple craft to distribute at the close of Lapsit.

1. As a parent I had wanted to create something for my child but never seemed to find the time. By having an item to show the adults, and explaining how to create it, I proved how little time it really did take to make something for their child.

2. There are lots of wonderful craft and activity books and we wanted to stress the ones that are useful for the pretoddler level of development.

3. Using craft items and tying them in with language development skills helped reinforce for the parents that the child has skills to master prior to reading.

4. Each week, by using a different craft we were able to demonstrate a different way adults and children can explore the world of language beyond the realm of books.

5. The librarian and parents could talk while the children were involved and relatively quiet.

6. The importance of adults interacting with their child verbally and physically was clearly demonstrated.

7. The library was raised a notch on the, "want list" of many of the adults. One comment was made that "It is great to see a public facility go through the bother of providing such a nice service for this age group. The one to two year olds are difficult to entertain and are nearly always overlooked in public services."

8. It gave the participants the impression that they were worth "something extra" and they valued the library staff that spent additional time preparing for their program. In using Lapsit in other environments, such as an alternative high school with teen parents, this may be the motivating factor for the adult and child to visit the library.

As stated the crafts are kept very simple and take less that 30 minutes to prepare for a class of 15 units (adult and child) per week.

Prior to distribution, it is important to remind adults about safety factors and that the child should not play with the item unsupervised. Although the craft is safe, stressing the importance of child and adult interaction with books and crafts can always be repeated. Each program during the series has a different craft and its use for language developments and interaction is explained.

## PUPPETS

The craft for the first program is usually some form of puppet. Because puppets are familiar to many adults, this initiates communication and are relatively easy to make. Puppets are also flexible to use and there are various types of puppets to make. I like to make finger or stick puppets for this project. When making stick puppets you can use a jumbo crafts stick (like a wide tongue depressor), glue or tape a circle of construction paper at one end with a sticker or happy face on it. Other types of sticks are mentioned such as wooden spoons, straws and even fingers.

Adults who don't like crafts or feel they cannot make things often find this is one thing they can make on their own at home. The fingerpuppets can be more involved and elaborate but as we said, it is better to keep it uncomplicated. Paper is another easy medium to use. An outline of a puppet that can be colored and cutout at home is sufficient.

Include with the pattern, words to an appropriate rhyme or song that can be used with it at home would be an added bonus for the child and adult. If time allows, the puppet could be cutout before the class and perhaps even laminated for durability. Felt, cloth, pompoms, etc. are materials that demand more prep time and paper fits most time limitations the best. Including resource books for other puppet patterns is a logical way to meet the needs of the motivated adult who wants to do more in the way of puppetry. Remember to mention how to use puppets for communication and interaction since some participants may think it is just a toy and not realize that it can be a useful tool to build language skills with.

## PICTURES CARDS

The craft for the second program is an item we call "picture cards" and one to each adult is given out at the class often when the book jackets are available. Materials needed are as follows:

1. blank index cards, size 4 inches by 6 inches are best, although smaller or larger work too.

2. bright pictures from bookjackets, catalogs, etc. that are simple and clear, stickers or shapes cutout from bright colored construction paper.

3. Clear contact paper.

Glue or stick the pictures/shape/sticker onto the index card. Place the card face down on the sticky side of the contact paper. Cut apart. The cards can be laminated instead if a machine is available but it is not necessary. The front of greeting cards may also be used but make sure there are no loose decorations or glitter that might prove to be dangerous to the child. These cards are very versatile and easy to use in language development. Stories can be told about the pictures, they can be put together as simple stories, children can sort them, put them in and out of containers (dishpans and shoeboxes work great for this), introduce children to descriptive words when describing them and more. Children are fascinated and will spend time examining and discovering their favorite picture card. These are not flashcards and should not be used as such. Bookjackets may be used for picture cards too as well as for posters, placemats, etc. Remind adults of places where posters might be hung and encourage them to talk to their child about what they see. Alternative places for picture cards and posters include by the changing table, the eating area, and the back of the child's door (a very boring spot if a child has to look at it before or after naptime). Picture cards may also be put together as a book although a magnetic photo album works better for this purpose. This craft has proven to be a favorite of the children and adults who attend Lapsit. It is inexpensive and not time consuming for the librarian to prepare and very easy to duplicate at home.

An alternative or adaptation of picture cards can be created by putting a sticker on a clean frozen juice lid, the kind that does not need to be removed with a can opener and has no sharp edges. These make interesting sounds when played with and can be "mailed" through a slot made in the top of a shoebox or plastic container. They are also large enough for tiny fingers to pick up enable the child to practice his or her small motor skills. Signal dots, the kind found in office supply stores, can be used and many games can be enjoyed. For example, sorting into piles by color, creating patterns, or just finding and naming colors.

## SQUISH BAGS

The craft for the third program is a favorite not only of the participants but the library staff as well. It is a finger paint bag or as it is known at our library a "squish bag." Materials needed are instant pudding mix, quart size ziplock bags and tape. To make it, use water as the liquid and add it to the pudding mix but less than is required, usually two thirds of the amount. Chocolate pudding mix makes wonderful "mud" and we have added food coloring to the vanilla to brighten it up. It is better to add the food coloring to the water prior to putting it in the mix. Orange works fine for programs in the fall, green in spring or March, yellow and red for summer. Use freezer bags because they are stronger than general storage bags, try to find ones without writing areas on them. Put about one quarter of a cup of the pudding into the bag and zip shut tightly after getting most of the air out of it. Tape around the bag using masking tape or whatever you have. Double the tape over the sides and make sure the corners are covered.

Basically this is a portable fingerpainting area that required no cleanup. Remind parents of safety factors and the importance of not leaving child unsupervised when playing with this especially if their child is still putting everything in the mouth. Drawing faces, shapes, letters whatever are fun and easy "lessons" with language that children and adults share when playing with this. Adults also appreciate its portability and the "pudding paint" does last a fairly long time.

## CREATING SOUNDS

The craft for the fourth program creates sound. Children this age are so aware of sounds and vibrations around them that it is fun to give them a simple craft we call a "shaker". It does make noise but not a very loud one. Materials needed are small containers such as a plastic egg, or clean prescription container with child-proof top, dry cereal or pasta, and stickers if desired. Fill the container partially with cereal or pasta, testing sound by shaking it after lid is replaced. Make sure the lid is secure and cannot be opened. It may be necessary to tape around middle of a plastic egg to keep it closed. Stickers can be used to decorate the container but it is optional. By using these "shakers," children and adults can learn about "fast and slow," "high and low," "soft and loud" by actual experience. Rhythm can be explored , songs enjoyed, and even the syllables that make up words can be used as sources for word games. A reminder of the importance of the adult's active participation with the child may need repeating when distributing this craft; that is what makes it a learning experience.

The final craft is somewhat involved and does take more preparation to create. It is a portable felt board that fits inside a quart-sized ziplock storage bag. This is a perfect size for fitting in a diaper bag or fair size purse. Materials needed are: quart size ziplock storage bags, felt, cardboard, glue, and tape. Cut the cardboard to fit inside the bag, about six inches by seven inches, making sure that it can go in and out of the bag easily. Cut the felt slightly smaller than the cardboard and glue onto cardboard; gluesticks work fine for this purpose. Tape around the edges making sure the felt and cardboard are both covered when the tape is doubled over the edge. Other pieces of felt may be cut into shapes to be used with felt board. Remember to keep the shapes simple and few in number, for example three circles of different colors, an orange pumpkin shape with black triangle shapes for eyes and mouth, or gingerbread man with red circle buttons. Keep the pieces large enough to be picked up by little fingers and larger than something to eat.

When it is put together, it is a self contained unit and easy to store pieces in. Shoeboxes and small pizza boxes work well also when felt is glued inside the cover and felt pieces can then be stored inside the containers. If this form demands more preparation than you have time for, recomend it for adults to make at home and be sure to have samples to show them. Other possible uses such as using the felt for assistance in making up stories or using picturebooks for resources helps the adult move on from a simple craft handout to the books on the library shelf.

Although, the initial investment of the librarian's time when developing the first set of handouts, displays and crafts may seem large, overall, preparation time becomes shorter as the librarian's familiarity and experience grows with running the Lapsit program and using the resources involved in it. Remember to keep in mind that the, number of children in your class does have a direct impact on how many items you need to prepare. It is this extra effort on the librarians part part that enables and encourages the adults to continue and extend the Lapsit experience at home with their children.

# RESOURCES FOR CREATING HANDOUTS, DISPLAYS, AND CRAFTS:

Cryer, Debby, Thelma Harms and Beth Bourland. *Active Learning for Ones.* Reading, Massachusetts: Addison-Wesley Publishing Company, 1987.

Hickman, Danell and Valerie Teurlay. *101 Great Ways to Keep Your Child Entertained While You Get Something Else Done.* Creative and stimulating activities for your toddler or preschooler. New York: Saint Martin's Press, 1992.

Lansky, Vicki. *Games Babies Play: from birth to twelve months*. Deephaven, MN: The Book Peddlers, 1993.

Kohl, MaryAnn F. *Scribble Cookies and Other Independent Creative Art Experiences for Children*. Mt. Rainier, MD: Gryphon House, Inc., 1985.

Martin, Elaine. *Baby Games: the joyful guide to child's play from birth to three years*. Pennsyhlvania: Running Press, 1988.

Miller, Daren. *Things to do With Toddlers and Twos*. Mass.: Telshare Publishers, 1984.

Striker, Susan. *Please Touch: How to stimulate your child's creative development through movement, music, art and play*. New York: Simon and Schuster, Inc., 1986.

# 5 SAMPLE PROGRAM

Planning programs for this age group allows lots of room for creativity, and personal talents and tastes. Depending on the presenter's preference they can be based on a theme or simply selected stories, rhymes and activities. Programs can be based on seasonal topics, concepts or a compilation of fun stories, rhymes and activities. The following five programs range from one using very basic materials to a more varied program using more diverse materials.

Each program should be planned to last approximately 20 to 25 minutes. Remember to allow the children time to absorb what is going on during the class and do not rush through the program. Plan on repeating the rhymes at least twice and if the children really want to hear a story again go right ahead but remember to be aware of the group dynamics. Depending on the group, the presenter can lengthen or shorten the duration of the program. When selecting materials always keep in mind that the materials need to be simple, at the very young child's level of understanding and interest. Keep in mind how the materials will flow from one to the next during the program and have a general idea of the pace you would like to maintain for your program. Remember, if the presenter enjoys the materials selected, the whole group will benefit as well. The enjoyment of the adult is infectious, and you are expressing your enjoyment not only for the benefit of the lesson at hand but molding an attitude for use by your adult participants.

## PROGRAM 1: 20 MINUTES IN LENGTH

### Opening Song

The More We Get Together

### Rhyme

Jack be nimble.
Jack be quick.
Jack jumped over the candlestick.
*(you can have children stand and jump up on the word "over", and can also have adults raise arms over child's head and catch them in a hug).*

### Rhyme

Hickory dickory dock.
*(Gently swing clasped hands in front of body)*
The mouse ran up the clock.
*(Raise arms over head)*
The clock struck one.
*(Clap hands once over head)*
The mouse ran down.
*(Lower clasped hands in front)*
Hickory, dickory, dock.
*(Gently swing clapped hands in front of body; for younger children the adult can actually hold the child and swing for first part of rhyme, when the clock strikes simply give a bounce and then swing gently again)*

### Song

Row, row, row your boat gently down the stream.
Merrily, merrily, merrily, merrily life is but a dream.
*(Sing this song three times. First at normal speed, then tell them to do the rhyme fast and then do it slow. After stating the speed, act out the rhyme in the following manner: children can sit on adult's lap or on floor between their legs holding hands, moving their arms to the rhythm and speed of the song.)*

### Story

*Mary Had A Little Lamb.* Hale, Sarah Josepha Accompanied by color photographs by Bruce McMillan. New York: Scholastic, Inc., 1990.

### Rhyme

Open, shut them.
Open, shut them.
*(Give a little clap.)*
Open, shut them.
Open, shut them.
*(Put them in your lap hands follow actions described in rhyme)*

### Song

Row, row, row your boat. (repeat from before)

### Story

*Brown Bear, Brown Bear, What Do You See?* Martin, Bill. Pictures by Eric Carle. New York: Henry Holt and Company, 1967, 1983.

### Song

If you're happy and you know it clap your hands. (follow actions described in song)

### Rhyme

> Patty cake, patty cake, baker's man.
> Bake me a cake as fast as you can.
> Roll it and pat it and mark with a B
> and there will be enough for baby and me!
> *(do appropriate actions)*

### Closing Song

The more we get together.

### Things to do at home

Visit a petting zoo. Look at magazines to find pictures of animals or watch a nature show on television. Talk to your child describing the animals and what they are seeing; include sounds that animals make. Cut pictures of animals out of magazines and make stick puppets out of them.

## PROGRAM 2: 20 to 25 MINUTES

### Opening Song

Use tape with familiar song while gathering group together.

### Rhyming Song

> Here's a ball for baby
> > *(form objects with hands)*. You can use taped music, recommend Little Songs For Little Me by Nancy Stewart. Mercer Island, WA: Friends Street Music, 1992.
> Here's a ball for Baby
> > *(hands make circle)*
> Big and soft and round.
> Here is baby's hammer, oh how he can pound.
> > *(bump fists together)*
> Here is baby's music, clapping, clapping so
> > *(clap hands)*

Here are baby's soldiers standing in a row
    *(Hold fingers upright)*
Here is baby's trumpet toot too-too, toot, too-too.
    *(pretend to play)*
Here is the way that baby plays at peek-a-boo
    *(cover eyes)*
Here's a big umbrella, keeps a baby dry.
    *(spread one hand over the other or over child's head)*
Here is baby's cradle, rock a baby bye.
    *(cradle arms together and rock)*

## Rhyme

    *(follow actions of rhyme)*
open, shut them, give a little clap.
open, shut them, lay them in your lap.

## Bouncing Rhyme

See my pony,
my jet black pony,
I ride him every day.
    *(do twice bouncing child gently on knee)*
When I give him oats to eat
trotting, trotting go his feet
    *(speed up bounce)*.
See my pony,
my jet black pony.
I ride him every day
    *(slow down to original pace)*

## Story

*Clap Hands.* Oxenbury, Helen. New York: Aladdin Books, 1987.

## Rhyme

There was a little turtle, he lived in a box.
    *(cup hands for box)*
He swam in the river and he climbed on the rocks
    *(pretend to swim and climb)*
He snapped at a mosquito,
he snapped at a flea,
he snapped at a minnow and he snapped at me!
    *(fingers and thumb snap shut like beak)*
He caught the mosquito,
he caught the flea,
he caught the minnow,
    *(clap hands on word caught)*
but he didn't catch me!
    *(point to self and shake head)*

### Story

*Pat the Bunny.* Dorothy Kunhardt. New York: Golden, 1940. Recreate book on separate pages to pass around.

### Rhyme

The Great Big Spider. A variation on Eency, weency spider. Children will find it easier to move their entire arms and legs rather than just their finger in the more traditional rhyme.

> The great big spider went up the water spout
> *(standing use arms and legs to create climbing motion)*
> Down came the rain and washed the spider out
> *(lower arms in front of body and swing gently back and forth)*
> Out came the sun and dried up all the rain
> *(raise arms in circle over head)*
> And the great big spider went up the spout again.
> *(arms and legs make climbing motions).*

### Rhyme

Patty cake, patty cake.

### Song

Old MacDonald had a farm. This is a good one to use the flannel board with cut-outs of farm animals.

### Story

*Where is Spot?* Eric Hill. New York: G.P. Putnam's Sons, 1980.

### Song

Where is Thumbkin. *(use only thumb)*

### Game

Ring around the rosie. Adult can hold child in arms and move in a circle. Adult and child can hold each others hands. This can also be done with the whole group holding hands but many children are hesitant and prefer not to hold a strangers hand.

### Things To Do At Home

Trace child's hand on paper. Let him or her play with different types of paper. Fingerpaint. Create a "touch bag" that contains different types of material and talk about what each one feels like. Use descriptive words whenever possible.

### PROGRAM 3: 25 MINUTES IN LENGTH

### Opening Song

The more we get together.

### Rhyme

Open Shut them.

### Story

*Just Like Jasper.* Butterworth, Nick and Mick Inkpen. Boston: Little, Brown and Company, 1989. Add sounds the toys would make each time.

### Rhyme

Hickory, dickory dock. Sway to beat and run fingers up child's chest, tap nose, run down chest.

### Action Rhyme

Tall as a tree
  *(stand up, arms stretched over head)*
Wide as a house
  *(arms stretched out from sides, feet apart)*
Thin as a pin
  *(feet together and arms at sides)*
Small as a mouse
  *(crouch on floor like mouse)*

### Rhyme

Jack in the box you sit so still.
Won't you come up?
  *(on floor crouched with hands hiding head)*
Yes I will!
  *(Pop up with arms over head)*

### Rhyme

This is the way the ladies ride prim, prim, prim.
  *(child on knee, gentle bounce)*
This is the way the gentlemen ride trim, trim, trim.
  *(child gets a stronger bounce)*
This is the way the farmer rides trot, trot, trot.
  *(rock child from one knee to other)*
This is the way the hunter rides gallop, gallop, gallop.
  *(child gets fast bounces)*

(use a horse puppet or make one out of paper roll with paper horse head taped to one end to resemble a stick horse. You may want to laminate horse's head to increase durability.)

## Story

*Spot Goes To The Farm.* Hill, Eric New York: Putnam, 1987.

## Rhyme

> Here is a bunny with ears so funny
> *(put hands by ears)*
> Here is his hole in the ground
> *(hold hand at waist arm makes hole shape)*
> When a noise he hears,
> he picks up his ears
> *(hands by ears)*
> And hops in his hole in the ground.
> *(Other hand hops in hole shape made by arm)*

## Rhyme

Jack be nimble, Jack be quick.

## Song

> If you're happy and you know it
> *(add action where appropriate)*
> Three little speckled frogs
> *(Use a flannel board with three frogs)*

## Story

*I Can Build A House.* Wantanbe, Shigeo. Illustrated by Yasuo Otomo. New York, New York: Philomel Books, 1983.

## Closing Song

The more we get together.

## Things To Do At Home

Give fingerpuppet pattern for frog puppet with words to Three Little Speckled Frogs to do at home. Talk to child about toys he or she has. Help your child build a house out of blocks or blankets. Visit a construction site and talk about what you see.

## PROGRAM 4: 25 TO 30 MINUTES

### Opening Song

The More We Get Together.

### Rhyme

Wiggle your fingers,
wiggle your toes,
wiggle your shoulders,
wiggle your nose.
*(wiggle appropriate body part)*

### Rhyme

*(Child gets bounced on knee gently, fast then slow)*
Bump'en downtown in my little red wagon,
Bump'en downtown in my little red wagon,
Bump'en downtown in my little red wagon,
Bump, bump, bump bump, bump bump.

### Rhyme

1,2,3,4,5
I caught a fish alive
*(clap hands around child five times then hug)*
6,7,8,9,10
I let him go again.
*(clap hands around child and then let go)*

### Story

*Brown Bear, Brown Bear, What Do You See?* Martin, Bill. Pictures by Eric Carle. New York: Henry Holt and Company, 1967, 1983.

### Action Rhyme

Two little monkeys jumping on the bed.

### Tickle Rhyme

Here comes a mouse. From Catch Me and Kiss Me and Say it Again by Watson.

### Stretch

Tall as a tree.

### Rhyme

Jack in the box.

### Rhyme

Cobbler, cobbler mend my shoe.
Give it one stitch,
give it two.
Give it three,
give it four,
and if it needs it give it more.
*(tap child's shoe then ask them to tap adult's shoe)*

### Story

*I Hear.* Isadora, Rachel. New York: Greenwillow, 1985.

### Rhyme

Humpty Dumpty.
*(Adult can gently bounce child on lap or sit on floor with knees raised. Bounce child by raising toes, then slid feet out so legs flat on floor when Humpty falls)*

### Song

Wheels on the bus.

### Story

*Grandfather Twilight.* Berger, Barbara. New York: Philomel Books, 1984.

### Closing Song

The More We Get Together.

### Things To Do At Home

Find different shoes and play games with them. For example: which shoe belongs to the child, adult, etc., or describe what shoe looks like, or sounds each shoe would make when walked in. Trace child's shoe. Don't forget boots, sneakers, slipper, etc..

**PROGRAM 5: 25 MINUTES.**

### Opening Song

If you're happy and you know it clap your hands.

### Rhyme

> Patty cake, patty cake baker's man
> Bake me a cake as fast as you can.
> Roll it and pat it and mark it with a B
> And there will be enough for baby and me.

### Rhyme

> These are *(child's name)* fingers *(wiggle fingers)*
> These are *(child's name)* toes *(wiggle toes)*
> This is *(child's name)* bellybutton *(tickle bellybutton)*
> Round and round it goes! *(draw circles on child's belly with finger)*

### Rhyme

> To market, to market to buy a fat hog.
> Home again, home again jiggety jog.
> To market, to market to buy a fat pig.
> Home again, home again jiggety jig.
> > *(bounce child gently on knees)*

### Rhyme

> Criss cross
> > *(trace large X on child's back)*
> Applesauce
> > *(tap child's shoulders)*
> Spiders crawling up your back
> > *(walk fingers up child's back)*
> Cool breeze
> > *(blow gently on child's neck and hair)*
> Tight squeeze
> > *(hug child)*
> Now you've got the shivers!
> > *(tickle child)*

### Rhyme

> 1,2,3,4,5, I caught a fish alive
> > *(clap hands around child, hug on "alive")*
> 6,7,8,9,10 I let him go again.
> > *(clap hands around child, then open arms)*

### Story

*Brown Bear, Brown Bear, What Do You See?* Martin, Bill. Pictures by Eric Carle. New York: Henry Holt and Company, 1967, 1983.

### Rhyme

Two Little Monkeys Jumping on the Bed.

### Rhyme

Round and round the garden goes the teddy bear.
*(use your finger to trace circles on child's palm, back or tummy)*
One step, two step, tickle him under there.
*(tickle child under arm or chin.)*

### Rhyme

Great big spider went up the water spout
*(Standing move arms and legs up and down)*
Down came the rain and washed the spider out
*(arms fall down to sides)*
Out came the sun and dried up all the rain
*(raise arms in circle over head)*
And the great big spider went up the spout again.
*(move arms and legs up and down)*

### Rhyme

Tall as a tree.
*(Stand up tall with arms over head)*
Wide as a house.
*(Stretch arms out to sides, feet apart)*
Thin as a pin.
*(Arms at sides, feet together)*
Small as a mouse.
*(Sink down to floor and crouch)*

### Rhyme

Jack in the Box you sit so still.
Won't you come out?
*(crouch on floor, head covered with arms)*
Yes, I will!
*(Pop up with arms over head)*

### Rhyme

Cobbler, cobbler, mend my shoe.
Give it one stitch, give it two,
Give it three, give it four and if it needs it give it more.
*(tap shoe while saying rhyme, second time ask child to tap your shoe.)*

### Story

*Where's Spot?* Hill, Eric. New York: G.P. Putnam's Sons,1980.

### Rhyme

Two little blackbirds sitting on a hill.
*(Hold up each hand)*
One named Jack the other named Jill.
*(Make beak shape by touching fingers and thumb or hold up one finger)*
Fly away Jack. Fly away Jill.
*(First one hand flies behind back, then other)*
Come back Jack. Come back Jill.
*(Hand flies back, then other)*

### Song

Wheels on the bus.

### Story

*The Little Mouse, The Red, Ripe Strawberry and the Big Hungry Bear.* Woods, Don and Audrey. New York Child's Play (International), 1990.

### Closing Song

The More We Get Together.

### Things To Do At Home

Make picture cards (sample given out as craft idea) let child sort and play with, then adult could describe what is shown on them. Look for letters such as street signs indicating bumps ahead for the letter "B" or stop signs for the letter "S".

# THEME PROGRAMS

When setting up programs that reflect themes you can incorporate some of your basic Lapsit materials and rhymes in it as well. The children will be exposed to new materials and yet still can recognize parts of the program also. Using an opening and closing song or rhyme helps create a pattern that the children will come to associate with the storytime and will respond by focusing their attention towards the presenter.

Using themes for a Lapsit program offers a structure that helps with concept reinforcement which you may want to include in your program. Themes also supply a framework on which the presenter can build their program and use it to enhance their creativity. For example, the theme "winter" can include books, rhymes, songs, etc. that cover snow, mittens, hats, boots and cold. Mother Goose rhymes are very useful in conjunction with themes since they cover a wide variety of subjects and concepts in a lively and fun manner.

An example of this is "Baa, baa, black sheep" which can be used for such themes as farms, sheep, colors, counting, etc. It is not necessary for all the materials selected for the program to reflect the theme since the very young child is only being introduced to these topics and concepts. Think of this program as an introduction rather than primarily a learning or teaching situation. Keep the theme in its place and do not limit the program materials to it alone. It is simply a guide, not something to be locked into. Use themes as a guide to create a fun language experience for the child and adult.

## BEARS

### Read Aloud

*Brown Bear, Brown Bear, What Do You See?* Bill Martin, Jr. Pictures by Eric Carle. New York H. Holt, 1967, 1992

*Bears*. Ruth Krauss. Pictures by Phyllis Rowad. New York Harper, 1948.

*The Little Mouse, The Red Ripe Strawberry, and The Big Hungry Bear*. Don and Audrey Wood. Illustrated by Don Wood. New York Child's Play (International), 1990.

### Rhymes To Use

1.  Teddy bear, teddy bear turn around.
    *(Standing up move in circle - child can also turn or be held by adult.)*
    Teddy bear, teddy bear, touch the ground.
    *(Touch fingers to floor)*
    Teddy bear, teddy bear, show your shoe.
    *(Bend and touch shoe)*
    Teddy bear, teddy bear, that will do.
    *(Clap hands three time on last three words.*

2.  Round and round the garden, goes the Teddy bear
    *(Use finger to draw circles on child's palm, tummy or back)*
    One step, two steps
    *(Walk fingers up child's arm, belly or back)*
    Tickle them under there.
    *(Tickle under child's chin or arm)*

### Songs

Bear Went Over The Mountain. This can be sung while marching or clapping to the beat. To make this into a fingerplay walk the fingers of one hand slowly up the opposite arm or that of child and down the other side.

### Things To Do At Home

Look for and point out to child things that begin with the letter "B". Trace the letter "B" on child's back or tummy. Play bouncing rhymes with child. Make a bear finger puppet or dancing puppet for child to play with.

### ME!

### Read Aloud

*Box With Red Wheels.* Maud and Miska Persham. New York: Macmillan Company, 1949.

*I Hear.* Rachel Isadora. New York: Greenwillow Books, 1985.

*How Do I Put It On?* Shigeo Watanade. Pictures by Uasuo Ohtomo. New York: Philomel Books, 1979.

*Clap Hands.* Helen Oxenbury. New York: Aladdin Books, 1987.

## Rhymes

1.  Patty cake, patty cake, baker's man.
        *(Clap hands in rhythm to rhyme)*
    Bake me a cake as fast as you can.
    Roll it
        *(Roll hands around each other)*
    Pat it.
        *(Clap hands together)*
    Mark it with a "B"
        *(Trace letter "B" on child's tummy)*
    And there will be enough for baby and me.
        *(Clap hands together, may also insert child's name instead of "baby")*

2.  Clap, clap, clap your hands as slowly as you can
    Clap, clap, clap your hands as quickly as you can.
        *(Do action indicated. Repeat with pound fists, shake hands, roll hands, pat face, etc.)*

3.  These are *(child's name)* fingers.
        *(wiggle fingers)*
    These are *(child's name)* toes.
        *(tickle toes)*
    This is *(child's name)* belly button, around and around it goes.
        *(use finger to draw circles around child's belly button.)*

4.  Shoe the Old Horse,
        *(Pat child's foot)*
    Shoe the old mare.
        *(Pat child's other foot)*
    Let the little pony run bare, bare, bare.
        *(Pat both feet together or pat child's bottom)*

## Songs

Head and Shoulders, Knees and Toes. *(Little songs for Little Me by Nancy Stewart.)*
Shake my Sillies Out. *(Raffi)*
When I was a baby. *(Baby Record by MacGrath and Smithrim)*
If you're happy and you know it.
Ring around the rosie.

## Things To Do At Home

Trace child's hand, adult's hand. Say child's name in conjunction with clothes, toys, meals, etc. When washing explain what you are doing and name body part. Dress child and ask for help. For example—hat on feet?, mitten on nose? Pants on head? The child will have fun showing adult the "right way" to get dressed. Play a naming game by describing what child is wearing and then give child a chance to guess who you are describing. Make a book about the child using photos or find pictures of child's favorite things in magazines and make into collage. Visit stores where the senses can be used such as a bakery, flower shop, fabric store. Help child learn how to describe feelings especially in actual situations. For example, if a child falls down ask him or her to describe what happened "Are you sad because it hurts?"

## CATS

### Read Aloud

*Will That Wake Mother?* Martha McKeen Welch. New York: Dodd, Mead, 1982.

*Who Said Meow?* Maria Polushkin. Illustrated by Ellen Weiss. New York: Bradbury Press, 1988.

*Just Like Jasper.* Nick Butterworth and Mick Inkpen. Boston: Little, Brown, 1989.

### Rhymes

1. Pussy cat, pussy cat, where have you been?
   I've been to London to see the Queen.
   Pussy cat, pussy cat, what did you there?
   I chased a little mouse under her chair.
       *(Child can be bounced gently on adult's knees.)*

2. Here comes a mouse, mousie, mousie, mouse.
       *(Wiggle fingers by child)*
   On tiny light feet and a soft pink nose, tickle, tickle, wherever he goes.
       *(tickle child)*
   He'll run up your arm and under your chin,
       *(run fingers up child's arm to chin)*
   Don't open your mouth or the mouse will run in!
   Mousie, mousie, mouse.
       *(Child will almost always open mouth, tap tongue or lips on last three words)*

3. Hickory, dickory dock.
       *(swing arms with hands together slowly in front of you or have adult hold child under arms and swing child gently)*

The mouse ran up the clock.
*(raise arms over head, lift child higher)*
The clock struck one
*(clap hands together once)*
The mouse ran down
*(lower arms or child)*
Hickory, dickory dock
*(swing arms or child back and forth)*

## Songs

Bought me a cat. (Little Songs for Little Me by Nancy Stewart)

## Things To Do At Home

Visit with a cat, make sounds like a cat. Read The Owl and The Pussy Cat by Edward Lear. Touch soft things and use words to describe them. Act out the three little kittens lost their mittens rhyme by showing mitten, then hiding mitten and finding it again.

## DOGS

### Read Aloud

*Where's Spot?* Eric Hill. New York: Putnam, 1980.

*Benny Bakes a Cake.* Eve Rice. New York: Greenwillow Books, 1981.

### Rhymes

1.  Log over leg, as the dog goes to Dover,
    When he comes to a wall,
    Jump! He goes over!
        *(bounce child on knee and big bounce on "Jump" or place child on lap, hold child's ankles, lift alternate legs over each other during rhyme then both on the word "jump" thus toppling child back against adult causing giggles.)*

### Songs

Oh where, oh where has my little dog gone?
I have a dog his name is Raggs.
*(Make silly motions to go with song)*

### Things To Do At Home

Visit a friendly dog and play with him, supervised by adult of course. Check out a book about dogs and look at all the various kinds. See how many kinds you and the child can see on the street.

## BUNNIES

### Read Aloud

*ABC Bunny.* Wanda Gag. New York: Coward, McCann, 1933.

*I Am A Bunny.* Ole Risom. Illustrated by Richard Scarry. New York: Golden Book, Western Publishing Company, 1963.

*Rabbit's Morning.* Nancy Tafuri. New York: Greenwillow Books, 1985.

### Rhymes

     Here is a bunny with ears so funny
       *(put hands by ears)*
     And here is his hole in the ground
       *(hold hand at waist making hole shape)*
     When a noise he hears, he picks up his ears
       *(hands by ears)*
     And hops in his hole in the ground.
       *(Other hand hops into hole shape at side)*
     Wiggle your fingers, wiggle your toes.
     Wiggle your shoulders, now wiggle your nose.
       *(wiggle body part)*

### Things To Do At Home

Make a bunny stick puppet or fingerpuppet to give out. Visit a petting zoo or pet store to meet a real bunny.

## FARMS

### Read Aloud

*Spot On The Farm.* Eric Hill. New York: Putnam, 1985.

*Mary Had A Little Lamb.* Sarah Josepha Hale. Photo-illustrated and afterword by Bruce McMillan. New York: Scholastic, 1990.

*Good Morning Chick.* Mirra Ginsburg (adapted from a story by Korney Chukovsky). Pictures by Byron Burton. New York: Greenwillow Books, 1980.

*Barnyard Tracks.* Dee Dee Duffy. Illustrated by Janet Marshall. Honesdale, Pa. Bell Books New York: distributed by St. Martin's Press, 1992.

*Spots, Feathers, and Curly Tails.* Nancy Tafuri. New York: Greenwillow Books, 1988.

*This is the Farmer.* Nancy Tafuri. New York: Greenwillow Books, 1994.

### Rhymes

1. Round and round the garden.
   *(see BEAR theme)*
   *(lower arms and rub tummy)*

2. This little piggy went to market.
   This little piggy stayed home.
   This little piggy had roast beef,
   and this little piggy had none.
   And this little piggy ran wee, wee, wee all the way home.
   *(Can be done the traditional way using child's fingers or toes. Try involving the child's whole body by jiggling arms, legs and finally belly.)*

3. This is the way the ladies ride.
   *(see Program in Sample Program section)*

4. Shoe the old horse, shoe the old mare.
   *(see ME! theme program)*

5. To market, to market to buy a fat pig.
   Home again, home again jiggety-jig!
   To market, to market to buy a fat hog.
   Home again, home again Jiggety-jog!
   *(bounce child on knees)*

6. Way up high in an apple tree,
   two little apples did I see.
   *(hold hands above head and make fists)*
   So I shook that tree has hard as I could.
   *(shake hands vigorously)*
   Down came the apples.
   Yumm, they were good! store and explore.

### Songs

1. Old MacDonald had a farm.
   *(can use a flannel board to illustrate while singing or have bag with various stuffed animals in it to bring out for each verse)*

2. The Farmer in the Dell.
   *(march to rhythm of song or use flannel board to illustrate)*

3. Mary had a little lamb.

### Things To Do At Home

Visit a farm or nursery. Plant a garden or a simple plant with your child. Dig in the dirt!

## HANDS

### Read Aloud

*My Hands Can.* Jean Holzenthaler. Pictures by Nancy Tafuri. New York: Dutton, 1978.

*Clap Hands.* Helen Oxenbury. New York: Aladdin Books, 1987.

*Here Are My Hands.* Bill Martin, Jr. and John Archambault. Illustrated by Ted Rand. New York: Holt, 1987.

*Piggies.* Don and Audrey Wood. Illustrated by Don Wood. San Diego: Harcourt Brace Jovanovich, 1991.

### Rhymes

1.   Open, shut them.

2.   Patty cake, patty cake.

3.   Clap, clap, clap your hands.

### Songs

1.   Wheels on the bus.
     *(Little Songs for Little Me by Nancy Stewart)*
     Note: you may want to limit the number of verses of this song to perhaps three or so. Roll hands around for the wheels, wave hands back and forth for wipers, tap child's nose or belly for horn, clap hands together for doors opening and shutting.

2.   Let everyone clap hands like me.

### To do at home

Trace child's hand and adult's hand. Clap at different speeds and levels of loudness. Give child a dishpan, box or pot to put cards or greeting cards in and out of. Blocks would work also instead of cards.

### Things To Do At Home

See how many things you can do with your hands: pick up a pencil, open a jar, make a fist etc.

## ZOO

### Read Aloud

*Dear Zoo.* Rod Campbell. New York: Four Winds Press, 1983, c1982.

*Sam Who Never Forgets.* Eve Rice. New York: Greenwillow Books, 1977.

*At The Zoo.* Douglas Florian. New York: Greenwillow Books, 1992.

*Little Elephant.* Miela Ford. Photographs by Tana Hoban. New York: Greenwillow, 1994.

### Rhymes

1. An elephant goes like this and that.

2. Ride a cock-horse, to Banbury Cross.

3. Two little monkeys jumping on the bed.

### Songs

1. All around the mulberry bush.

2. Mama's taking us to the zoo tomorrow.
   *(Peter, Paul and Mommy by Peter, Paul and Mary)*

### Things To Do At Home

Visit a zoo, check out books about animals from the library. Make an elephant fingerpuppet to play with. (Act like some of the animals at the zoo using actions and sounds)

## TOYS

### Read Aloud

*The Ball Bounced.* Nancy Tafuri. New York: Greenwillow Books, 1989.

*Mother's On Lap.* Ann Herbert Scott. Drawings by Glo Coalson. New York: McGraw-Hill, 1972.

*Just Like Jasper.* Nick Butterworth and Mick Inkpen. Boston: Little, Brown, 1989.

*Now We Can Go.* Ann Jonas. New York: Greenwillow, 1986. (This book can be made into a flannel board story or use props to tell story taking items out of box and putting them into a bag.

### Rhymes

1. Here's a ball for baby.
   *(form objects with hands)*
   Here's a ball for baby.
   Big and soft and round.
   Here is baby's hammer, see how he can pound.
   Here are baby's soldiers, standing in a row.
   Here is baby's music, clapping, clapping so.
   Here is baby's trumpet, tootle-tootle-oo.
   Here's the way that baby plays at peek-a-boo!
   Here's a big umbrella to keep the baby dry,
   Here is baby's cradle, rock a baby by.

2. Jack in the box, you sit so still
   *(Kneel on floor with arms Won't you come out? covering head)*
   Yes, I will!
   *(Pop up with arms in air on "Yes")*

3. Johnny hammers.
   *(Make hammer motions with one fist, then two. Depending on children add foot movement also)*
   Johnny hammers one hammer, one hammer, one hammer.
   Johnny hammers one hammer all day long.
   *(Continue with hammers with two hammers, etc.)*

4. Bump'en downtown in my little red wagon.
   Bump'en downtown in my little red wagon,
   Bump'en downtown in my little red wagon,
   Bump, bump, bump, bump, bump, bump!
   *(Bounce child on knee. Go fast, slow whatever. This is a rhyme I use to illustrate how I forgot the words and just put in the word bump, still fun to say and do)*

### Songs

1. I'm a little tea pot.

2. Ring around the rosies.

### Things To Do At Home

Make a picture book of toys and let child "read" it. Can be made from a magnetic photo album. Give child an old catalog to learn about paper and how it tears. Give the child different types of paper to give them a sense of what they feel like and how they can handle them. (This activity should be done under adult supervision.)

## NIGHT

### Read Aloud

*Goodnight Moon.* Margaret Wise Brown. Pictures by Clement Hurd. New York: Harper and Row, 1975, c1947.

*Ten, Nine, Eight.* Molly Bang. New York: Greenwillow Books, 1983.

*Grandfather Twilight.* Barbara Berger. New York: Philomel Books, 1984.

*Goodnight Owl.* Pat Hutchins. New York: Macmillan, 1972.

*I Hear.* Rachel Isadora. New York: Greenwillow, 1985.

### Rhymes

1.  Twinkle, twinkle little star.
    *(while saying or singing this rhyme wiggle fingers above head)*
    How I wonder what you are?
    *(put hand on chin)*
    Up above the world so high
    *(point above head)*
    Like a diamond in the sky.
    *(draw circle in air above head)*
    Twinkle, twinkle little star. How I wonder what you are.
    *(wiggle fingers above head)*

### Songs

1.  Two little monkeys jumping on the bed.
    *(hold one hand palm up the other hand has two fingers tapping it)*
    Note: With children this age it is sometimes easier to limit the number to two or three in this kind of song. Easier for the children to do)
    Two little monkeys jumping on the bed.
    *(two fingers jump on open hand)*
    One fell off and bumped his head.
    *(tap head)*
    Mama called the doctor and the doctor said.
    *(one hand makes circle in the air as if dialing, other hand to ear.)*
    "No more monkeys jumping on the bed!"
    *(wag finger up and down)*

### Things To Do At Home

Create a bedtime ritual including a story to read aloud. Look at the night sky and talk about what you see. Make up a good night rhyme such as "Good night, sleep tight, see you in the morning bright." Use dark colored paper and make stars on it with chalk; make a bookmark of dark paper and put star stickers on that. Take your child on a night walk or perhaps visit a planetarium.

## DUCKS

### Read Aloud

*Five Little Ducks.* Raffi. Illustrated by Jose Aruego and Ariane Dewey. New York: Crown, 1989.

*Have You Seen My Duckling?* Nancy Tafuri. New York: Greenwillow Books, 1984.

*Ducks Fly.* Lydia Dabcovich. New York: Dutton, 1990.

### Rhymes

1. Mr. Turkey and Mr. Duck.
   *(start with hands behind back, one hand is Mr. Turkey, the other is Mr. Duck, One hand comes out first)*
   Mr. Turkey went out one day in bright sunshiny weather.
   He met Mr. Duck along the way, they stopped to talk together.
   *(hands make beak shape and gobble and quack to each other)*
   Gobble, gobble, gobble!
   Quack, quack, quack!
   Gobble, gobble, gobble!
   Quack, quack, quack!
   *(hide hands behind back, then Mr. Duck sneaks back for the last word)*
   And then they both went back . . . Quack!

2. Two Little Black Birds
   *(hold up both hands or just one finger on each)*
   Two little blackbirds sitting on a hill.
   One named Jack, the other named Jill.
   *(raise one hand, then the other)*
   Fly away Jack, fly away Jill
   *(hide hands behind back)*
   Come back Jack, come back Jill.
   *(hands fly back)*

### Songs

The one little duck with the feather on his back.
Five little ducks went out one day.

### Things To Do At Home

Visit a duck pond. Make duck sounds. Walk like a duck. Look for feathers not only outside but other places such as hats, pillows, etc.

## WINTER

### Read Aloud

*The Happy Day.* Ruth Krauss pictures by Marc Simont. New York: Harper Collins, 1949.

*Tom and Pippo in the Snow.* Helen Oxenbury. New York: Aladdin Books, 1989.

*How Do I Put It On: getting dressed.* Shigeo Watanabe. New York: Harper Collins, 1979.

### Rhymes

1. Warm hands warm. Do you know how?
   If you want to warm your hands, blow on them now.
   *(rub hands together while saying rhyme, then blow gently)*

2. Snow is falling down, shhh.
   Snow is falling down, shhh.
   Softly, softly, very softly
   Snow is falling down, shhh.
   *(start with hands raised and slowly lower while wiggling them. On word "shh" touch finger to lips in hushing motion. Hands may be raised at the beginning of each line)*

3. Grandma's glasses
   These are Grandma's glasses
   *(use hands to make circles around eyes)*
   This is Grandma's hat
   *(put hands on head, clasp hands together)*
   This is the way she folds her hands and puts them in her lap
   *(do actions)*
   These are Grandpa's glasses
   *(use hands to make circles around eyes)*

This is Grandpa's hat
*(hands on head, point upward)*
This is the way he folds his arms just like that!
*(cross arms)*

## Songs

Where is Tumbkin?
*(may want to do just thumb and pointer finger with this age group)*
Here's a ball for baby
*(see TOYS theme program)*

## Things To Do At Home

If it is winter play in the snow or at least outside. Look at ice, frost, other signs of cold weather. Talk about the clothes for outside play. Let child dress up a doll or play toy for the cold weather.

## THINGS THAT GO

## Read Aloud

*Freight Train.* Donald Crews. New York: Greenwillow, 1978.

*Zip, Whiz, Zoom!* Stepanie Calmenson. Boston: Little, Brown and Co., 1992.

*Cars.* Anne Rockwell. New York: Dutton, 1984.

## Rhymes

1.  I'll drive a dump truck.
        *(Little Songs for Little Me by Nancy Stewart)*
        *(slap thighs to beat while singing or chanting)*
    I'll drive a dump truck, dump truck, dump truck
    I'll drive a dump truck all day long.
        *(can repeat with school bus, airplane, choo choo train, etc. Enhance this by holding up pictures of different vehicles each time.)*

## Songs

1.  Wheels on the bus.

2.  Here is the choo choo train.
        *(Little Songs for Little Me by Nancy Stewart)*
    Here is a choo choo train,
        *(bend arms at elbows)*
    chugging up the tracks.
        *(rotate arms in rhythm)*

Now it's going faster now the bell is ringing,
Now the whistle blows
*(hold fist near mouth and blow)*
What a lot of noise it makes, everywhere it goes!
*(cover ears and shake head)*

## Things To Do At Home

Use a box or furniture to create a make believe car, train, etc. Go for a car ride. Try to find an airplane when it flys overhead. Visit an airport or train station.

## PROGRAM FOR INFANTS AND ADULTS

When the basic concept and outline of the Lapsit program have been mastered and the presenter feels comfortable with the flow of the program, it is possible to adapt the outline to serve other groups of people. Infants and their caregivers, older toddlers or preschoolers and adults can all be served by changing the emphasis of the basic four part outline you have become familiar with

1. General introduction and background,
2. Lapsit storytime,
3. Adult Education, and
4. Discussion period.
5. In order to do this let us examine how each group can be served by using the four basic components of the Lapsit outline.

When adapting the Lapsit for infants or children who have not yet discovered mobility you must keep in mind that the program will be aimed primarily at the adults. The rhymes can be the more familiar Mother Goose ones and the adult participants must be encouraged to do the actions for the child. You can do this by having the adult hold the child and adapting the actions according to the child's abilities. To illustrate by using the following rhyme:

"Hickory, dickory, dock".
Many librarians use this rhyme in preschool storytime and it is often done standing up. "Hickory, dickory, dock". (Action group stands, individuals clasp their two hands together and swing them gently back and forth to resemble a large standing clock)
"The mouse runs up the clock"
*(Action clasped hands are raised above head)*
"The clock struck one
*(Action clap hands together one time)*

"The mouse runs down"
  *(Action clasped hands are lowered in front)*
"Hickory, dickory, dock
  *(Action clasped hands are swung gently back and forth again).*

Obviously this action is too complex for infants to perform. Have the adult run his or her fingers up the child's body, touch the child's nose on the word one and then tickle their fingers down the child's body. Another way is for the adult to hold the child and walk to the beat of the rhyme. The action rhymes can also be interspersed throughout the informational portion of the program to add clarification. After explaining how the children develop awareness of their own body you can use the following rhyme.

"These are *(child's name)* fingers,
these are *(child's name)* toes,
this is *(child's name)* belly button,
around and around it goes" *(circle child's tummy)*
  as an example of how this concept can be reinforced with a fun language activity.

The following outline was used for an infant/parent workshop presented in 1992 in King County, Washington that and can be used as a guide to recreate your own.

## BABIES AND BOOKS

### I. Basic Introduction and Welcome.

A.  Presenter name, background, etc.
B.  Individuals introduce themselves and child (child's age is also helpful). This helps people in the group get "settled in".

### II. Guideline and Rules

A.  Don't expect the children to sit still or be quiet.
B.  Do expect the adults to participate to the best of their ability.
C.  To relax and have fun.

### III. Infants Plus a Caring Adult Equals Fun

A.  When to read to a child? Children arrive in the world ready to learn. Since a baby can see only about 14 inches away much of the first learning is done by sound. A child who is talked to, sung to, read to and communicated with will learn about the world and people who surround him or her and want to be a part of that world too. By starting early you are encouraging communication and bonding between the very young child and the adult.

B. Why read to children as infants? This gives a good foundation for developing other skills such as listening, comprehension, etc. The child develops a familiarity with words, rhyme patterns, that gives them something to imitate as they develop communication skills.

C. How to read to a child. Relax—children are uncritical and the child can sense your attitude towards books. Read in a way that won't overstimulate the child and provides a chance to understand the rhyme and word. For example, read the shopping list, say a nursery rhyme, read a street sign. Be expressive and aware of the interaction between you and the child. Be a role model for your child as a reader.

D. Remember each family is unique as is each child. Make up your own rhymes, songs stories and experiences to share together.

## IV. What Is a Book?

A. As Adults we know what a book is but a child does not.
   1. Paper? What is it, it rips, different kinds — let the child experience paper.
   2. Book? We know about beginning, middle and end of stories—child does not.
   3. Pages? Adults know how to turn pages without ripping them and one at a time but child does not. Give them catalogs to practice.

B. Types of books available.
   1. Quality picture books. (show samples and explain why they are good for this age group.
   2. Board books.
   3. Participation books such as lift the flap or pat the cat (touch and feel books).

C. What books do: introduce the child to concepts, colors, sounds, and the world around him or her, helps children become aware of themselves, and develops listening and comprehension skills. This can only be done with the guidance of an adult who is willing to involve his or herself with the child and the book. Otherwise the book is just an object.

## V. Introducing the Child to the World of Words

Within this section include why children love rhymes and rhythm. Children have been surrounded with rhythms during the nine months in the womb. Rhythm can soothe a child, help distract him or her from an undesirable action or behavior. They become familiar to the child who can enjoy them and anticipate change. Rhymes are fun and easy to remember especially in the middle of the night. Forgotten words can usually be replaced with little difficulty using one's imagination. Many of these rhymes, songs, etc. are on tapes that can be used by non-singers at home or even in the car.

    A. Awareness of self.
       Patty-cake, patty cake.
       Head and shoulders, knees and toes.
       These are *(child's name)* fingers.
    B. Daily activities.
       Shoe the old horse. Use when changing child's diaper.
       Rub a dub dub. Giving the child a bath.
       Rain is falling down, splash. During bath time.
    C. Tickles.
       Round and round the garden goes the teddy bear.
       Criss Cross Applesauce.
       There was a little man.
    D. Bounces.
       Ride Baby Ride.
       To market, to market.
    E. Story Rhymes.
       This little piggy went to market.
       Hickory dickory dock.
       All around the mulberry bush.
       Row, row, row your boat.

## VI. Library Services and Materials Available

    A. Services such as requesting books by phone, interlibrary loans, send materials directly to the patron's home, hours library is open, number of libraries available to them, etc.
    B. Materials covering such topics as basic child development *Please Touch* by Susan Striker, consumer reports, videos, picturebooks of all types, personal concerns—for example crying, discipline, going back to work, etc.—newspapers and magazines, books of fingergames, and things to do with the child in the area.

### VII. Conclusion

Books are special and lots of fun. By enjoying this activity with your child, you are sharing and teaching your child your values and morals. Read what you enjoyed as a child. Use the library to "try out" books you may want to add to your own family library. You are introducing your child to vocabulary, art, themselves and their world by using books. You are also giving the child a good foundation to build on in the future. In sharing books with your child you are also sharing yourself and creating a bond that is very important between family members. You (the parent) are doing a great job in bringing up your child and we are glad we can help.

# VARIATIONS OF ADULT WORKSHOPS

Adult workshops are aimed at a wide variety of people. It is necessary to keep in mind the audience you intend to address. There is a wide variety of parents and caregivers for the very young child. The format needs to meet the needs of the group. Should the presenter be the librarian or would it be better to have a specialist do the presentation with the librarian hosting or moderating. How much time should be allotted for questions and answers, can demonstrations be given, would an interpreter be helpful and should the presentation be formal or casual re all important to take into consideration.

Teen parents, adults who are just learning English as a second language, first time parents who are older and have been more career oriented, parents who were never read to a children, single parents and parents who are physically separated from their extended family support group all have parenting needs. The childcare provider has other needs with larger numbers of children to attend to. No matter what the workshop includes, be it child development, networking to locate resources, how to find jobs, one of the most important goals the librarian needs to aim for is that of helping the adult realize

1. How important it is to read and talk with their child,
2. Be a role model in reading not only with their child but for themselves,
3. Use language and books throughout the day and
4. To keep it simple, fun and to relax.

# RESOURCES

To create easier workshop, audio-visual materials can be incorporated into the program, and a booktalk/library awareness presentation can be added to it. There are numerous videos and films available of very good quality. Using the media as the core of the program enables you to tailor your booktalk to the group you are with and to the purpose you intend the program to serve. Here are a few recommended titles

*Choosing the Best in Children's Video.* (Features Christopher Reeve as host.) American Library Association Graphics, American Library Association, 1990, 35 minutes. Video.

*Drop Everything and Read.* (Features Fred Rogers, Jim Trelease, and others.) Films for the Humanities and Sciences, 1986. 28 minutes. 16mm film and video.

*Read to Me Libraries, Books and Your Baby.* Greater Vancouver Library Federation, 1987. 15 minutes. Video.

*What's So Great About Books?* Orlando Public Library, 1977. 15 minutes. 16mm film.

Additional titles can be found in Ellin Greene's book (*Books, Babies and Libraries: Serving Infants, Toddlers, Their Parents and Caregivers,* along with a directory of producers and distributors).

For teen-parents, for example, you may want to stress baby care, services the library supplies and how to assist them in locating support groups. For childcare providers you may want to inform them of specialized services your library provides specifically for groups. The King County Library System in Washington has developed a program called Beginning With Books where a children's librarian visits the childcare facility for a certain number of weeks to do actual storytimes and instruct the caregivers in how to use literature in their daily program. After the visits are completed they can then check out boxes that contain stories, puppets, resources on various topics they would cover during the year. The materials are compiled for them and they now know how to make better use of it.

Presentations to childcare providers can include resources for working with children in groups and they can also contain materials that can help support their clientele. For example, working parents, separation anxiety, things to do in and around the area the families live in, discipline, self esteem for children, storytime materials that work and the fact that language and stories can be throughout the day from storytime, clean-up time, naptime and all the time often needs to be brought to their attention.

There are three books that are very useful when developing a program that fits your library's goals and requirements. *First Steps to Literacy* contains library programs for parents, teachers and caregivers. The caregivers are not only professional but include high school students as well. Created by the Preschool Sevices and Parent Education Committee of the Association for Library Service to Children this book supplies the outlines for seven different programs including ones for expectant parents, grandparents and adults not trained as children librarians but working with children in the public library. *Running A Parent/Child Workshop: A How-To-Do-It Manual* (Neal-Schuman Publishers, 1995) by Sandra Feinberg and Kathleen Deerr of Middle Country Public Library, or the Mastics-Moriches-Shirley Community Library , concentrates on the parent and child together and emphasizes parent involvement as early as possible.

It is a five week program and covers and introduction or what the program is about, speech and language, child development and play, nutrition and finally physical fitness and movement. This may be useful in helping you decide important areas to cover and supplies lots of information if the area of library service to the very young child becomes a major goal of your library. It is available from:

Children's Services Department
Biblios, Middle Country Public Library,
101 Eastwood Blvd.,
Centereach, N.Y. 11720

The final resource is *Books, Babies and Libraries* by Ellin Greene. This text has information which includes early childhood development, parent education, program models, resource materials, information from the 1989 invitational conference Babies, Books and Libraries, jointly sponsored by the New York Public Library and New York University and detailed lists of books, audio-visuals, organizations computer information, magazines, and networking with other child-serving agencies.

Programs are only part of the library and literature experience for the adult and very young child. Librarians in a sense are always doing programs whether for a group or one on one while giving reader's advisory help. By encouraging parents or caregivers with very young children to use the library and become acquainted with its services helps all who are involved develop their literacy abilities.

Children are exposed to the beginning skills necessary for communication and eventually reading. The adult creates a shared experience with the child, encouraging dialog and practice time to reinforce his or her own literacy skills. The programs incorporate fun activities, simple stories, rhymes and songs in addition to learning experiences for all the participants to enjoy together.

# RECOMMENDED READING LIST FOR LIBRARIANS

## BOOKS

Bos, Bev. *Before the Basics: Creating conversations with children.* Roseville, California: Burton Gallery, 1983.

Butler, Dorothy. *Babies Need Books.* New York: Atheneum, 1985.

Carlson, Ann. *Early Childhood Literature Sharing Programs in Libraries.* Hamden, CT.: Shoe String Press, 1985.

Cryer, Debby, Thelma Harms and Beth Bourland. *Active Learning For Ones.* Reading, Masssachuseetts: Addison-Wesley Publishing Company, 1987.

DeSalvo, Nancy. N. *Beginning with Books: Library Programming for Infants, Toddlers and Preschoolers.* Hamden, Connecticut: Shoe String Press, 1993.

Elkind, David. *The Hurried Child: Growing Up Too Fast Too Soon.* Reading, Massachusetts: Addision-Wesley Publishing Company, 1981.

Feinberg, Sandra and Kathleen Deerr. *Running A Parent/Child Workshop: A How-To-Do-It Manual for Librarians.* New York: Neal-Schuman, 1995.

Greene, Ellin. *Books, Babies and Libraries: serving infants, toddlers, their parents and caregivers.* Chicago: American Library Association, 1991.

Lamme, Linda Leonard. *Growing Up Reading.* Washington, D.C.: Acropolis Books Ltd.,1985.

MacDonald, Margaret Read. *Booksharing: 101 Programs To Use With Preschoolers.* Library Professional Publications, 1988.

Marino, Jane and Dorothy F. Houlihan. *Mother Goose Time Library: Programs for Babies and Their Caregivers.* New York: H. W. Wilson Company, 1992.

Miller, Karen. *Ages and Stages: developmental descriptions and activities. birth through eight years.* Chelsea, Mass.: Telshare Pub. Co., 1985.

Miller, Karen. *Things to do With Toddlers and Twos.* Chelsea, Mass.: Telshare Publishers, 1984.

National Council of Teachers of English by its Committee on Literature in the Elementary Language Arts. *Raising Readers: A Guide to Sharing Literature with Young Children.* New York: Walker and Company, 1980.

Preschool Services and Parent Education Committee, Association for Library Service to Children. *First Steps to Literacy: Library Programs for Parents, Teachers, and Caregivers.* Chicago: American Library Association, 1990.

Quiggt, Claudia. *Baby Talk: How to make it Work!* Illinois, Rolling Prairie Library System, 1989.

Striker, Susan. *Please Touch: how to stimulate your child's creative development.* New York: Simon and Schuster, 1986.

Winkel, Lois and Sue Kimmel. *Mother Gooose Comes First: An annotated guide to the best books and recordings for your prechool child.* New York: Henry Holt and Company, 1990.

## AUDIO-VISUAL MATERIALS

**Beginning with Excellence - An Adult Guide to Great Children's Reading.** Produced in cooperation with *The Horn Book.* (audio cassettes)

**Literacy and Families: The Library Link.** ALSC/AASL/YASD. American Library Association, 1988. (audio cassettes)

MacGrath, Bob and K. Smithrim. **The Baby Record.** Kid's Records, 1983. (record, cassette)

**Read to me: Libraries, books and your baby.** Greater Vancouver Library Federation. (Video).

**Ring Around Reading: Infants and the Literacy Experience.** ALSC, 1987. ALA preconference, 1987. (audio cassettes)

**STAR PARENTING: The resource for parenting toddlers ages one through three. A positive and practical approach to effective parenting.** Dr. Rober Fox and Theresa Fox. Star Parenting Inc., 1990. (audio cassettes)

Stewart, Nancy. **Little Songs For Little Me: activity songs for ones and twos.** Mercer Island, WA: Friends Street Music, 1992. (cassette)

## ARTICLES

"Read Me a Story." Jim Trelease. Parents, February/91. page 106.

"Raising a Reader." teaching your child the joys of language. Joan Vos. American Baby, October/89. Page 64.

"Saying It Louder." Dorothy Butler. School Library Journal, June/89. page 18.

"Sitting Pretty: Infants, Toddlers and Lapsits (helping parents introduce their babies to books). Debbie Jeffery and Ellen Mahoney. School Library Journal, April/89. page 37.

"Pittsburgh's Beginning with Books Project." J. Locke. School Library Journal, February/88. Page 22.

"The Parent/Child Workshop: A unique program." Sandra Feinberg. School Library Journal, April/85. Page 38.

"Parents, New Babies and Books." Helen Cannon and Joyce Dixon. School Library Journal, January/78. Page 68.

## RECOMMENDED READING LIST ON CHILD DEVELOPMENT

Ames, Louise Bates, Frances L. Ilg and Carol. C. Haber. *Your One Year Old: the fun loving, fussy 12 to 24 month old.* New York: Delacorte, 1982.

Balter, Lawrence, with Anita Shreve. *Dr. Balter's Child Sense: Understanding and handling the common problems of infancy and early childhood.* New York: Simon and Schuster, 1985.

Brazelton, T. Berry. *Toddlers and Parents: A declaration of independence.* New York: Dell, 1986.

Dombro, Amy Laura and Leah Wallach. *The Ordinary Is Extraordinary: How children under three learn.* New York: Simon and Schuster Inc., 1988.

White, Burton L. *The First Three Years of Life. Revised edition.* Englewood Cliffs, NJ: Prentice-Hall, 1987.

## HANDOUT SAMPLES

Handouts, as previously stated, can be as simple or elaborate as the presenter cares to make them. Here are the handouts that I have created to get you started.

### Welcome Sheet or "Rules" Sheet

At the first class everyone receives a welcome sheet, a list of fingergames that will be used, and the business card of the librarian. If no business card is available, use the library's open hours or information flyer and print the presenter's name on it. Having a contact name is important for the busy caregiver and indicates that someone will respond to their inquiries.

**Figure A-1: Welcome Sheet**

# Welcome Everybody —
# How Do You Do?!

This is a special library time just for you!

Here are a few "rules" to keep in mind when our program is in session. Your cooperation will help all who attend to enjoy and profit from these sessions.

1. Parent participation is key to the success of this program! You are best equipped to help your child focus on our activities. Please join in the activities and show your child it's fun!

2. Please put toys and food away. They distract your child and other children. If bottles, blankets or other not-to-be-parted with items are necessary we will work with it. Breastfeeding is also ok if need be.

3. You will probably have lots to share with the other parents. Time for this interaction has been set aside after the program. We would like to do the program first, when the children are fresh. The room is free for your use until 8:00pm.

4. If your child is crying loudly or otherwise distracting the group, or in another sense loosing control, please feel free to step out and "regroup". Talk to me if you are unsure or concerned about your child's behavior.

5. **RELAX!** It is not expected that your child will sit still and participate in each activity. Our goal is to have fun with rhymes, songs books, and other language-building play.

**Figure A-2: Lapsit Fingergames and Songs**

## Fingergames And Songs Being Used In The Program

Here are a few of the fingergames and songs we will be using during this program. Please try them out at home with your child.

**Clap Your Hands:**
Clap your hands one, two, three
   (clap hands on one, two, three)
Clap your hands, just like me
   (clap hands on last three words)
   (Other verses can be roll your hands, wave your hands, pat your nose,etc.)

**Criss Cross Applesause:**
Criss, cross, applesauce
   (draw an X on child's back with finger, tap shoulders on las word)
Spiders running up your back
   (walk fingers up child's back)
Cool breeze
   (blow gently on child's neck and back of head)
Tight squeeze
   (give child a big hug)
Now you've got the shivers!
   (tickle child gently)

**Jack in the Box:**
Jack in the box you sit so still
   (kneel on floor with head covered by arms)
Won't you come out? Yes, I will!
   (pop up on last phrase)

**Open, Shut Them:**
Open, shut them. Open, shut them.
   Give a little clap.
Open, shut them. Open, shut them.
   Lay them in your lap.
   (Do appropriate hand motions)

**Shoe The Old Horse:**
Shoe the old horse. (pat child's foot)
Shoe the old mare. (pat child's other foot)
Let the little pony run, bare, bare.
   (pat child's bottom)

**Wiggle Your Fingers:**
Wiggle your fingers,
wiggle your toes,
wiggle your shoulders,
now wiggle your nose.
   (wiggle appropriate part of body)

**Ride Baby Ride:**
(Bounce child on knee by raising the heel of your foot. Can do this at any pace and as often as child likes. To end say Whoa and give child hug)
Ride baby ride.
Ch, ch, ch, ch ch, ch.
Ride that horsey ride.
Ch, ch, ch, ch, ch, ch.
Whoa . . .

**Johnny Hammers One Hammer:**
Johnny hammers one hammer, one hammer, one hammer.
Johnny hammers one hammer all day long.
   (Pump one hand up and down or tap one hand on lap)
Johnny hammers two hammers, two hammers, two hammers.
Johnny hammers two hammers all day long.
   (pump both hands up and down or tap both hands on lap)

**Round and Round:**
Round and round the gardern goes the teddy bear
   (trace circle on child's hand, back or tummy)
One step, two step, tickle her/him under there!
   (Move fingers up arm,tickle under chin or arm)
Teddy Bear: (do appropriate motions)
Teddy bear, tedddy bear, turn around.
Teddy bear, teddy bear,touch the ground.
Teddy bear, teddy bear, show your shoe.
Teddy bear, teddy bear,that will do.
   (clap hand on last three words)

**Two Little Blackbirds:**
Two little blackbirds stting on a hill
   (hold both hands up in air)
One named Jack, the other named Jill.
   (hold up one hand,then the other)
Fly away Jack, fly away Jill.
   (move hands behind back)
Come back Jack, come back Jill.
   (bring hands back into front of body)

**Head and Shoulders, Knees and Toes:**
Head and shoulders, knees and toes.
Knees and toes. Knees and toes.
Head and shoulders, knees and toes.
Eyes, ears, mouth and nose.
   (touch appropriate part of own body or child's body)

Don't forget to use your favorite song, play peek a boo, the alphabet song, count out loud, dance with your child, create your own rhymes, enjoy all kinds of music together.

**Figure A-3: Lapsit Program Review**

# Lapsit Program Review
(This is usually handed out at the last program.)

Here is the list of books used during the program, craft ideas to recreate at home, other titles you may want to enjoy, and tips to keep in minds when looking for books to share with you child.

Lapsit Program
*(Month/Year)*

## Books Used

*Brown Bear, Brown Bear.* Bill Martin Jr. New York: Holt, 1983.
*Box With Red Wheels.* Maud and Miska Petersham. New York: Macmillan, 1949.
*Where's Spot.* Eric Hill. New York: Putnam, 1980.
*The Little Mouse, the Red, Ripe Strawberry and the Big, Hungry Bear.* Don and Audry Wood. Child's Play, 1984.
*I Hear.* Rachel Isadora. New York: Greenwillow Books,1985.
*Grandfather Twilight.* Barbara Berger.New York: Philomel, 1984.

## Craft Ideas

### Stick Puppets

Tongue depressor or ice cream stick small circle of colored paper taped on to one end with a decorative sticker on it.

### Picture Cards

Unlined index cards with a picture glued on it and then covered with clear contact paper.

### Finger Paint Bag

Instant pudding (chocolate or vanilla colored with food coloring) sealed in a ziplock bag (best to use heavy duty) with tape around all the sides.
Pudding can be made with water and use only half the required amount.

### Felt Board

Felt cut into shapes can be placed on small felt board (cardboard cut 7inches by 6 inches, covered with flannel or felt).
Store in ziplock bag.
Inside of small box or even individual pizza box can be used also by gluing felt on inside of cover and store pieces in bow.

**Figure A-4: Selecting Books**

*Things to keep in mind when selecting books for your young child:*

- Illustrations that are simple and clear, easy to distinguish seem best.

- Stories about what the child sees and experiences tend to be favorites for this age group.

- The child is learning to turn pages so books made with durable materials (for example vinal or board books) allow them to read indendently till this skill is mastered.

- Children at this age often develop favorite stories so select books you won't mind reading again and again.

- Magazines and catalogs are bright and colorful for the child to browse through. If pages rip when they are ''reading'' they will learn about paper and master the skill of turning pages without ripping them. It is less expensive then letting them practice with a picturebook.

*The Toddler's Bookshelf:*

- *Bathwater's Hot* by Shirley Hughes.
- *Goodnight Moon* by Margaret Wise Brown.
- *Marmalade's Nap* by Cindy Wheeler.
- *Pat the Bunny* by Dorothy Kunhardt.
- *Sam Who Never Forgets* by Eve Rice.
- *Shopping Trip* by Helen Oxenbury.
- *Taste the Raindrops* by Anna Hines.
- *The Very Hungry Caterpillar* by Eric Carle.
- *Where's Spot?* by Eric Hill.

**Note:** Some titles are best used when read to the child by an adult instead with a group. Enjoy them!

**Figure A-5: Art and Crafts With Your Child**

# Art Activity Recipes

Children in this age group can be very creative. Because many children still put things in to their mouths, it is better not to use recipes that demand a great deal of salt, the use of tempera as a coloring agent, or have alum as an ingredient. Here are some simple and fast art recipes for you to try.

## Playdough

1 cup flour
½ cup salt
2 teaspoons cream of tarter

Mix these together and add to: 1 cup of boiling water, 2 teaspoons oil, food coloring. Cook, stirring constantly, over medium heat for three to four minutes until it form a ball. Store in a plastic bag or container. Can be kept in refrigerator.

## Playdough

(This dough is a little firmer and holds its shape better)

four cups of flour
1 cup of salt
4 tablespoons of cooking oil or shortening
1½ cups of water (add more a little at a time if needed)
Food coloring (about one fluid ounce for dark color) or powdered tempera paint.

Add food coloring to water for ease in mixing. If tempera is used, mis with flour and salt. Mix dry ingredients together and add liquid until pliable, like a piecrust. Store in a plastic bag this will keep, depending on use, for about a month. If it gets too sticky, just add more flour.

## Glue or Cornstarch Paste

One of the easiest pastes to make is a mixture of flour and cold water. It is a good non-poisonous past. It will not keep, so make a small amount at a time. Food coloring may be added if you wish.

Cornstarch paste is made by mixing three tablespoons of cornstarch in one cup of cold water, then boiling the mixture until it thickens. When cool it can be used as a paste. This will separate in time, just reheat and cool before using again.

## Fingerpaint

This art material is something children really like to get involved with so if you feel comfortable food is the best fingerpaint to use for the younger pretoddler. Cranberry sauce, applesauce, yogurt, canned pumpkin pie mix, sour cream, are a start then just use your imagination.One half cup cornstarch, three fours cup cold water, boil in a pan. Add two cups of boiling water which has food coloring in it if so desired, cook until it boils clear. Cool mixture and then use.

## Oatmeal dough

1 cup of flour
2 cups of oatmeal
1 cup or water

Cook over medium heat, stirring constantly for three minutes. Knead well. When cool, store in plastic zip lock bag.

**Figure A-6: Evaluation Form**

# Evaluation Form

Please fill out this evaluation and return to the library in attached envelope by (date). Thank you!

1. How old is your child?

2. How many lapsit programs did you attend:     All     Half     One

3. What did you like the best about the program?

4. What did you like least about the program?

5. Did the program meet your expectations?

6. Have you used any of the ideas presented at home?

7. Did you think the materials were suitable for the age range?

8. Was the time relatively convenient?

9. If offered again, would you attend this class?

10. Sugestions and/or comments:

## EVALUATIONS

Evaluations are useful to improve and enhance your program. Using them enables the participants to add their imput and gives a different perspective to the program. By gathering statistics and opinions with the evaluation, the librarian can justify offering this program when necessary to the administration or community. I have found that the adults who attend the Lapsit program very insightful and supportive. Keeping the evaluation simple and concice is important. Include a self-addressed envelope with the evaluation to encourage returning it.

# All About...  Parenting

Your King County Library can help you answer the many questions about pregnancy, childbirth and parenting that arise.

Even before the child is born, parents need information on pregnancy (618.24) and related health issues. Should you breast-feed or perhaps use the Lamaze birthing method? Perhaps adoption is the appropriate means of increasing your family. (362.734) In any event, baby names will have to be considered (929.4).

With the arrival of the child comes a myriad of questions. Child health, safety, nutrition and fitness are primary concerns. These can be found in titles such as **The Parent's Pediatric Companion** (618.92), **Foods for Healthy Kids** (613.2088), and **Be a Frog, a Bird, or a Tree (J613.7).**

Along with the responsibilities of parenting come the joys. Sharing books can begin at an early age. **A to Zoo: Subject Access to Children's Reading Books** (RO11.62), booklists compiled by King County Library System, Jim Trelease's **Read-Aloud Handbook** (372.6), Nancy Larrick's **Parent's Guide to Children's Reading** (010) and **Children's Toys and Books** (649.5) are all ways to find appropriate materials.

Traveling with children can be enhanced by books such as **Discover Seattle with Kids** (917.9777).

Parents are concerned about their child's safety as they grow up. Books on child abuse such as **Private Zone** (362.7044) and **Protect Your Children** are helpful for sharing between parent and child. There are also titles on discipline: Dobson's **Dare to Discipline** (649.1) and the **One-Minute Scolding** are two among many. There are valuable

manuals to have in the home for baby-sitters including The Baby-sitter's Handbook (Y649.1).

As the child grows, toilet training becomes a major achievement. Books to help the parents cope can be found in 649.6. School success and helping your child to read are also important, many titles are in 649.58 and the 372's.

Stages of development and how to parent can be found in the 155.4's such as **Child Development** by the Gesell Institute and **Between Parent and Child** by Ginott.

For parents with teenagers, special questions arise, particularly in the area of sex education. Two books on the subject are the **Family Book about Sexuality** (612.6007) and **Sex Education Begins at Home** (649.65). These offer straightforward advice and ways to handle this sensitive issue. The King County Library System also has a list of books, films and video cassettes called "Adolescence: Choices and Changes" and a list of video cassettes called "That Teen Show."

You can also check out the video cassette **Mr. Rogers Talks with Parents about School** (VT372.18). Check the complete non-fiction video list for the wide range of parenting videos.

*The Children's Librarian and the Reference Librarian are available to answer your questions and to help you find information on this subject. Please ask.*

**ⓂKING COUNTY LIBRARY SYSTEM**
1992

# BOOKS AND RESOURCES FOR PARENTS

These titles are useful to create displays, bibliographies and help the adult become aware of titles, media, and names of those who create materials for this age group. These lists can also be used to help the librarian examine the library's collection of materials for the very young child and adult.

## MORE BOOKS FOR THE VERY YOUNG CHILD AND ADULT TO ENJOY TOGETHER:

Boynton, Sandra. *Moo, Baa, La La La.* New York: Simon and Schuster, 1982. (this author has other board books available also)

Chorao, Kay. *The Baby's Good Morning Book.* New York: Dutton, 1986.

_____. *The Baby's Lap Book.* New York: Dutton, 1977

Crews, Donald. *Freight Train.* New York: Greenwillow, 1978.

Emberley, Ed. *Sounds.* (First Words board book series, other titles: *Animals, Cars, Boats, and Planes and Home*) New York: Little, Brown and Co., 1987.

Gag, Wanda. *ABC Bunny.* New York: Coward McCann, 1933.

Hale, Sarah Josepha Hale. *Mary Had a Little Lamb.* Ill. by Brucce McMillan. New York Scholastic, 1990.

Hill, Eric. *The Spot books.* New York: G.P. Putnam's Sons, 1986. (flap book series)

Hoban, Tana. *What Is It?* New York: Greenwillow Books, 1985. (board book, others in series include: 1,2,3 a first book of numbers: Tana Hoban has other board books and photo-illustrated books that work with this age group as well)

Hughes, Shirley. *Bouncing.* Cambridge, Massachusetts: Candlewick Press, 1993.

_____. *Giving.* Cambridge, Massachusetts: Candlewick Press, 1993.

_____. *Bathwater's Hot.* New York: Lothrop, Lee and Shepard, 1985.

Isadora, Rachel. *I Hear.* New York: Greenwillow, 1991 (rev.ed.), 1985.

_____. *I See*. New York: Greenwillow, 1991 (rev.ed.), 1985.

_____. *I touch*. New York: Greenwillow, 1991 (rev.ed.), 1985.

_____. *Babies*. New York: Greenwillow, 1990.

Krauss, Ruth. *The Carrot Seed*. New York: Harper, 1945.

Lindgren, Barbro. *Sam's Ball*. New York: Morrow, 1983. (series of books that feature a little boy's activities. Small in size)

Lionni, Leo. *What?* New York: Pantheon Books, 1983 (board book, others in series are *When?, Where?, Who?*)

Ormerod, Jan. *This Little Nose*. New York: Lothrop, 1987.

_____. *Reading*. New York: Lothrop, Lee and Shepard, 1985.

_____. *Messy Baby*. New York: Lothrop, Lee and Shepard, 1985.

_____. *The Saucepan Game*. Lothrop, Lee and Shepard, 1989.

Oxenbury, Helen. *All Fall Down*. New York: Aladdin, 1987. (board book)

_____. *Clap Hands*. New York: Aladdin, 1987. (board book)

_____. *Tickle, Tickle*. New York: Aladdin, 1987. (board book)

_____. *Tom and Pippo books*. New York: Aladdin, 1989. (there are a number of books with these two friends in them.)

Raffi. *Five Little Ducks*. New York: Crown, 1989.

Rice, Eve. *Benny Bakes a cake*. New York: Greenwillow, 1981.

_____. *Sam Who Never Forgets*. New York: Greenwillow, 1977.

Scott, A. *On Mother's Lap*. New York: McGraw-Hill, 1992, 1972.

Welch, M. *Will that Wake Mother?* Dodd, Mead, 1982.

Wood, Audrey. *The Napping House*. HBJ, 1984.

_____. *Piggies*. HBJ, 1991.

# IN ADDITION TO MOTHER GOOSE

De Angeli, Marguerite, ed. *Marguerite de Angeli's Book of Nursery Rhymes.* New York: Doubleday, 1953.

dePaola, Tomie. *Tomie dePaola's Mother Goose.* New York: Putnam, 1985.

Lear, Edward. *The Owl and the Pussycat.* New York: Putnam, 1991. Illustrated by Jan Brett.

Lobel, Arnold. *Random House Book of Mother Goose.* New York: Random House, 1986.

Prelutsky, Jack. *Read-Aloud Rhymes for the Very Young.* New York: Knopf, 1986.

Ra, Carol, comp. *Trot, Trot to Boston: Play Rhymes for Baby.* New York: Lothrop, Lee and Shepard, 1987.

Sieveking, Anthea. *Polly Put the Kettle on and Other Rhymes.* Hauppauge, New York: Barrons Educational Series, 1991. (there are three other board books in this series reflecting other Mother Goose rhymes.)

Watson, Clyde. *Catch Me and Kiss Me and Say It Again.* New York: Philomel, 1978.

# HELPING PARENTS CREATE READERS

Butler, Dorothy. *Babies Need Books.* New York: Atheneum, 1980.

_____. *Reading Begins at Home.* Portsmouth, New Hampshire: Heinemann Educational Books, 1979.

Cullinan, Bernice. *Read to Me: Raising Kids Who Love to Read.* New York: Scholastic, 1992.

_____. *First Steps Toward Reading.* (Parenting Services) New York: Time-Life Books, 1987.

Lamme, Linda Leonard. *Growing Up Reading: Sharing With Your Children the Joys of Reading.* Herndon, Virginia: Acropolis Books, 1985.

McEwan, Elaine. *How to Raise a Reader.* Elgin, Illinois David C. Cook, 1987.

National Council of Teachers of English. *Raising Readers: A Guide to Sharing Literature With Young Children.* Walker, 1980.

Trelease, Jim. *The New Read-Aloud Handbook.* New York: Penguin Books, 1989.

## AUDIO MATERIALS

Jim Trelease's **Turning on the Turned-off Reader.** 90 minute audio cassette version of the popular lecture and film on reading aloud. For information write:
Reading Tree Productions, Ins
51 Arvesta Street
Springfield, MA 01118
(413-782-5839)

**Beginning with Excellence - An Adult Guide to Great Children's Reading.** Produced in cooperation with *The Horn Book.* Transripts for the three cassette audio included. For information:
Sound Advantage
22 Hawthorne Road
Wayland, MA 01778
(1-800-545-3765)

# ACTIVITIES TO DO TOGETHER

Fisher, John. *Toys To Grow With: Infants and Toddlers, Endless Play Ideas That Make Learning Fun.* New York:"A Perigee book", 1986. Co-Creator, Johnson and Johnson Develpment Toys.

Lansky, Vicik. *Games Babies Play.* Wayzata, Minnesota: Book Peddlers, 1993.

Miller, Karen. *Things to do With Toddlers and Twos.* Chelsea, Massachusetts: Telshare Publishing, 1984.

Martin, Elaine. *Baby Games: The Joyful Guide to Child's Play From Birth to Three Years.* Running Press, 1988.

Striker, Susan. *Please Touch: How to Stimulate Your Child's Creative Development Through Movement, Music, Art and Play.* New York: Simon and Schuster, Inc., 1986.

## HELPING YOUR CHILD LEARN

Baldwin, Rahima. *You Are Your Child's First Teacher* Berkeley, California: Celestial Arts, 1989.

Baron, Naomi S. *Growing Up With Language: How Children Learn to Talk. Redding,* Massachusetts: Addison-Wesley, 1992.

Belliston, Larry. H*ow to Raise a More Creative Child.* Argus Communication, 1982.

Bos, Beverly. *Before the Basics: Creating Conversations With Children.* Roseville, California: Turn the Page Press, 1983.

Dombro, Amy Laura and Leah Wallach. *The Ordinary Is Extraordinary: How Children Under Three Learn.* New York: Simon and Schuster, 1988.

# PARENT CONCERNS

Ames, Louise Bates. *Your One-Year-Old: the fun-loving, fussy 12 to 24 month old.* New York: Delacorte Press, 1982.

Anderson, Eugene. *Self Esteem for Tots to Teens: Five Principles for Raising Confident Children.* New York: Simon and Schuster, 1984.

Balaban, Nancy. *Learning to Say Goodbye: Starting School and Other Early Childhood Separations.* New American Library, 1987.

Balter, Lawrence. *Who's In Control?: Dr. Balter's guide to discipline with out combat.* New York: Poseidon Press, 1988.

Bettelheim, Bruno. *A Good Enough Parent: A Book on Child Rearing.* New York: Random House, 1987.

Brazelton, T. Berry. *Working and Caring.* Reading, Massachusetts, Addison-Wesley Pub., 1985.

Brazelton, T. Berry. *Toddlers and Parents: A Declaration of Independence.* New York: Delacorte Press, 1989.

Cherry, Clare. *Parents, Please Don't Sit on Your Kids: a parents guide to non-punitive discipline.* David S. Lake, 1985.

Dobson, James. *The Strong-Willed Child: Birth Through Adolescence.* Wheaton, Illinois: Tyndale House, 1978.

Lansky, Vicki. *Getting Your Child to Sleep- and Back to Sleep: tips for parent of infants, toddlers and preschoolers.* Emeryville, California: Publishers Group West, 1991.

Kellerman, Jonathan. *Helping the Fearful Child: a parent's guide to everday and problem anxieties.* Norton, 1981.

Leach, Penelope. *Your Baby and Child: From Birth to Age Five.* New York: Random House, 1989.

Sears, William. *Creative Parenting: how to use the attachment concept to raise children successfully from birth through Adolescence.* Dodd, Mead, 1987.

Sprague, Maxine. *Positive Parenting Strategies.* Learning Center Press, 1986.

Weisberger, Eleanor. *When Your Child Needs You: a parent's guide through the early years.* Chevy Chase, Maryland: Adler and Adler, 1987.

Williams, Lynn , Henry S. Berman and Louise Rose. *The Too Precious Child: the perils of being a super-parent and how to avoid them.* New York: Atheneum, 1987.

Sanger, Sirgay. *The Woman Who Works, the Parent Who Cares: a revolutionary program for raising your child.* Little, Brown, 1987.

## AUDIO MATERIALS:

Star Parenting: The resource for parenting toddlers age one through three. A positive and practical approach to effective parenting by Dr. Robert Fox and Theresa Fox. Star Parenting, 1990. Four Audio Cassettes and workbook. Topics include: parent role, child develpment, positive parenting, setting limits, toilet training, going to bed, communication techniques and response techniques. Parenting is not for cowards.

# VIDEOS

## FOR THE ADULT:

Choosing the Best in Children's Video: a guide for parents and everyone who cares about kids. Hosted by Christopher Reeve. American Library Association Video, 1990.

Read to Me: Libraries, books and your baby. Greater Vancouver Library Federation, 1987.

What every baby knows. T. Berry Brazelton hosts four programs: "most common questions about newborns,infants and toddlers"; "the working parent"; "a guide to pregnancy and childbirth"; and "on being a father". Upbeat Videos, 1984 and 1985.

Winning at Parenting . . . without beating your kids. Barbara Coloroso. From the series: Kids Are Worth It! A Pannonia International Film, 1989.

**FOR THE CHILD AND ADULT TO ENJOY TOGETHER**

**A Young Children's Concert.** Raffi and the Rise and Shine Band. A & M Video,

**Baby Songs.** Hi-Tops Video, 1987

**More Baby Songs.** Hi-Tops Video. 1987.

**Raymond Briggs' The Snowman.** Snowman Enterprises, Ltd., 1982.

# VARIETIES OF MATERIALS

Select three or four titles to illustrated the variety of materials available in a certian topic. Here are two such selections.

### Poetry:
*The Owl and the Pussycat.* Written by Edward Lear. Illustrated by Jan Brett. New York: G.P. Putnam's Sons, 1991.

Illustrated by Paul Galdone. Boston, Massachusetts: Clarion Books, 1987. (Board book version available)

### ABC books:
(Remind them to use the alphabet song or say them in a chant.)

*ABC Bunny* by Wanda Gag. New York: Coward McCann, 1933.
*26 Letters and 99 Cents* by Tana Hoban. New York: Greenwillow, 1987.

*Chicka Chicka Boom Boom* by Bill Martin and John Archambault. Illustrated by Lois Ehlert.

# INDEX

Linda Ernst has been a children's librarian for the past 17 years. She has served communities in Illinois and Washington. Ernst is currently employed by the King County Library System in Washington. Actively serving very young children and their caregivers for the past seven years has been an important part of her job and one of the most enjoyable. Just as parents are encouraged to keep it simple and start early to expose their children to the world of language and literature, Ernst offers assistance in applying this knowledge to the area of library service to very young children. She has given Lapsit training workshops for the King County Library System, Seattle Public Library, and Everett Public Library in Washington. In 1995 Ernst will present the Lapsit workshop at the Washington Library Association Conference. *Lapsit Services for the Very Young Child: A How-To-Do-It Manual* is Ernst's first book. Linda L. Ernst lives in Bellevue, Washington with her husband and daughter.